D1584338

LEARNING TO LOVE

FRANK ADVICE FOR
YOUNG CATHOLICS

LEARNING TO LOVE

FRANK ADVICE FOR YOUNG CATHOLICS

Marc Oraison, M.D.

translated by
André Humbert

DEUS BOOKS
PAULIST PRESS
(Paulist Fathers)
New York, N. Y.

COVER DESIGN: Claude Ponsot

Printed and bound in the United States
of America by Our Sunday Visitor Press

CONTENTS

A # 105

CONTENTS

INTRODUCTION

THE FULLY-GROWN MAN or woman is one who really has left his adolescence behind. In spite of what some authors seem to imply, it is more or less easy to overcome a bad childhood. But it is rather difficult to put to rest the memories of a bad adolescence. The first six years of life are critical, to be sure, and where serious emotional disturbances are found the culprits are to be looked for here. But most of us who are reasonably sane —who hold jobs, have friends, assume responsibility and, let us admit, seem to enjoy living—whatever our early origins, came through the later growing-up process quite successfully. A man may hate authority because of Oedipus, but it is more likely that most of the rebels and malcontents with grey beards had conflicts with pop or mom at sixteen or seventeen that were never quite resolved in their favor. So they keep on fighting. A contemporary wife may, if she reads the right books, blame her sexual frigidity on bad toilet training, but more likely the real causes need not be traced that far back.

What I am saying really is what everybody knows— that teen-age living is highly important in the mature development of the human personality. It is during these critical five or six years that the person discovers whether or not he or she can go it alone from here on in, whether or not the mythical silver cord of dependence has really been cut.

It is during these years, too, that the person really discovers and explores the meaning of his sexuality for the first time. What happens here can affect him for a lifetime. Or her.

The end result of this seminary of life is either graduation to self-confidence in one's own worth as male or female and a capacity to deal wholesomely and correctly with members of the opposite sex, or perversion of one kind or another.

Therefore, one of the most important phases of education is education during adolescence for future manhood or womanhood. If the history of every person is a kind of dialogue between our mysterious God and this mysterious creature called man, then the unveiling of both God and man begins during these critical years.

That is why *Learning to Love* is the right book for the right people at the right time and written by the right man. Frank advice to young Catholics is critically necessary for them, particularly in our present sex-loaded culture. And Marc Oraison, priest, theologian, medical doctor, and experienced teacher has just that happy combination of faith, scientific knowledge, and common sense to blend the right mixture of Catholic teaching on a vitally important subject.

Perhaps the last paragraph of his book explains best what he tried to do and what, in the judgment of the present writer, he did admirably.

Marc Oraison writes in conclusion: "Hopefully this book will help young people to know and use the forces of human dignity and love as we see these forces through modern scientific knowledge and through God's revealed word. Each young man and woman needs instruction in spiritual self-denial in order to bring the drives of sexual instinct into line with the attitudes of "togetherness" that we need for married life. Self-denial is a matter of personal choice, but this choice and the subsequent moral effort should certainly be made a lot easier by the fact that enlightenment now comes from two different sources: faith and science. These two, each supporting the other, can dispel anxiety, clarify what is happening, and give us some idea of things to come."

The value of this book is that it combines so admirably the conclusions of science and religion. The youth is given to know all there is to be known about God's design for man's sexual nature; and he receives from Marc Oraison's intelligible faith the guidelines for its proper use. To have accomplished this happy result is no mean achievement for any author.

One sees too many attempts, even among Catholic writers, to look only to the world for direction on sexual matters, as if the two thousand years of Christian teaching were all dark ages.

One hears everywhere in America—among self-styled intellectuals, in high-priced magazines, and among half-educated practitioners on street corners—that the old sexual morality is on its way out. The revolt against the sexual morals of Christianity is applauded in high places and in low. The norm that sexual intercourse belongs to marriage alone is considered no longer binding. As a matter of fact, to speak of fornication any more in some circles is rather gauche; one rather refers to "the importance of adequate sexual adjustment by adult and responsible unmarried males and females."

We in America do have to deal with some startling facts. The number of illegitimate births in the United States has tripled since 1940. We have more high-school girls dropping their education because of pregnancy than ever before. Half the women married are under twenty; the young marriages have a high rate of divorce;

and already 13 million children are growing up in broken homes.

These data must be balanced by the fact that many teen-agers grow up in stable homes, with loving care, and in solidly moral communities. But, even here, these youngsters must deal, as we never did, with a culture saturated with sex stimuli.

At all events, young people must learn early how to deal with their own sexuality. This is especially important for Catholics. One cannot train the married people of 1980 with the motivation and data that comes from the world of 1880. Let us face facts: much of that indoctrination hoped to accomplish its end result through taboos and social pressure. Neither of these will work in a world where free and intelligent commitment to a way of life is considered preferable to blind conformity.

Catholics must hold certain moral truths even against the power of world and flesh. But now they must be taught the reasons for their importance, what revelation teaches on these matters, and the significance of chastity for the young, whether they get married or remain single. Because so much is left to the individual today, there is need for a larger understanding and a richer spiritual life!

Here is where Marc Oraison makes a valuable contribution to the Christian formation of Catholic youth. He takes all that the world says about sexuality—its goodness, its developing power, its importance to healthy manhood and womanhood—and shows how these values are best preserved within a Christian framework. He certainly makes no concessions to the world on moral standards. It will become very obvious to the thoughtful reader that the capacity to deal with the problems of marriage will be developed for the most part during the adolescent, and presumably celibate, years.

I consider Marc Oraison's *Learning to Love,* coming as it does from the pen of a man acknowledged to be a leader in this field, to be a book that can be called sex education at its best.

GEORGE A. KELLY
Director,
FAMILY LIFE BUREAU
ARCHDIOCESE OF NEW YORK

FOREWORD

IT IS NOT REALLY so long ago that the realities of sexual life became the subject of scientific study. The science of physiology came into its own only around the beginning of the last century. The kind of psychology interested in the flesh-and-blood man and not in man in the abstract wasn't born until Freud opened the way to research in the evolution of emotions. Until then, it had not been known that the sexual instinct, like all mental activity, follows a long evolutionary course begun at birth.

This short book springs from an elementary principle: the clearer the blueprint, the better finished the work will be. It wants nothing more than to present to young men and women all-important, up-to-date knowledge about sexuality. Young people should not have to be experts in biology, nor in the psychology of the unconscious, but they do have to know how to be themselves more deeply and effectively.

In these few pages, then, we should make things as clear as possible, in words that just about everyone will understand. Two main themes, both of them essential, will emerge: first, that the manifestations of sexuality in adolescent living are obviously important and must be clearly understood; secondly, that this sexuality is *only one among many aspects* of the birth and growth of personality. To claim that sexuality is a leading villain, or to show it as the prime and only cause in the drama of personality development, is an error of some so-called moralists. Psychologists, on the other hand, certainly do not try to reduce everything to sex. This book is about sex, but sex as just one part of our lives.

I: ABOUT THE BODY

1

ABOUT THE BODY

WOMAN

AN IMPORTANT THING about the woman's genital system is that it's mostly hidden inside the body. This fact has an effect on woman's psychology—a subject we'll be talking about again later. The diagram here shows woman's genital system.

The *uterus* is a hollow muscle, like the heart. Because the uterus, or womb, is hollow, it can hold the product of conception—the ovum, or "egg," and later the fetus, the unborn baby.

A tube (the *oviduct*) extends out from each of the two upper corners of the uterus. Each tube ends in a kind of flared fringed opening (the *ampulla*). Near it lies the *ovary*. The ovaries produce the eggs and also hormones (or internal secretions which affect the whole body).

The opening in the lower part of the uterus, called the *cervix*, or neck, protrudes out into another passage, the vagina, which in turn opens out into the *vulva*. The vulva is the name of the outer structures: folds of skin, two on each side, an inner pair, the *labia minora*, an external pair, the *labia majora*, and at the front upper part the *clitoris*. The clitoris can become erect, much like the male sex organ, the penis. The clitoris is the principal center of sexual excitation and feeling. A thin membrane called the *hymen* partially closes the opening of the vagina, and usually lasts as long as a woman has not had complete sexual intercourse. The existence of the unbroken hymen is sometimes considered proof of virginity, and so is called the *maidenhead*.

Now let's see how all these parts function. First we'll look at what goes on under usual circumstances, when no sperm from the male has entered the woman's body, then we'll see what happens in the female when the woman is impregnated and fertilization occurs.

The female system without impregnation. Unlike that of the male, the female genital organism functions in

FEMALE GENITAL SYSTEM

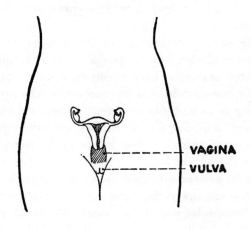

VAGINA
VULVA

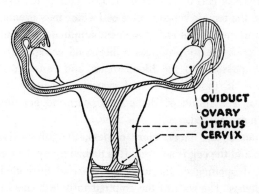

OVIDUCT
OVARY
UTERUS
CERVIX

cycles, but the beginning of its activity comes at a time of life common to both sexes—puberty—that period which is such a crucial stage in the growth of the human person.

The entire outer surface of the woman's ovary is made up of what may be thought of as a stockpile of potential sex cells. Each twenty-eight days, approximately, one of these cells becomes active. This cycle of activity is to be repeated constantly from the time of puberty until the woman reaches age fifty—on the average, of course—a time known as the *menopause*, or the "change of life."

At the beginning of each cycle, one cell in the outer layer of the ovary "blossoms out." It develops into a tiny liquid-filled pocket, the *follicle*. Within this pocket lies the sex cell as it first develops. This is the egg, or *ovum*, the female reproductive cell which may eventually be fertilized by the living element supplied by the male. This pocket also produces a hormone called *estrogen* which passes into the bloodstream and causes certain changes in the whole sexual system, especially in the uterus. The lining of the uterus begins to get thicker and more folded.

After twelve days, more or less, the follicle bursts open, and the egg is set free. It is picked up by the flared, fringed opening of the tube, and carried through it to the uterus. The wall of the emptied follicle forms into a small yellow mass (the *corpus luteum*) which acts as a temporary gland and gives off a second hormone, *progesterone*, into the bloodstream. Progesterone, in its turn, acts on the uterus. It causes the lining of the uterus to thicken still more, increase its folds, and fill with a nutritive substance much like sugar. At the same time, progesterone quiets the muscular part of the uterus so that it doesn't contract. With such preparations of the uterus, if the ovum should become fertilized, it would find all conditions already ideal for attaching itself to the wall of the uterus and growing there.

When the ovum doesn't encounter any male sex cell it soon dies and is dissolved. The *corpus luteum* survives for about fourteen days and then stops producing the progesterone. On or about the twenty-eighth day of the cycle, the muscle part of the uterus, no longer paralyzed by progesterone, contracts. The mucous membrane lining of the uterus, thick and gorged with blood and sugar, becomes loose and peels off. Loose flakes are discharged from the vagina in the form of tiny bits of waste mixed in with a slight flow of blood. This discharge is called *menstruation*, or the *period*, the *menses*.

The young girl who has reached puberty will have, along with this discharge, minor symptoms such as fleeting pains, physical and mental uneasiness. The periodic activity of the ovary affects the entire person. Woman's basic sexuality is related to everything else much more than in man.

The bursting of the ovarian follicle, or ovulation,

occurs at only one particular moment in the cycle. A woman is not continuously fertile. The functional life span of the male reproductive cells is usually no more than two days. So, fertilization is probably possible only during the two days before the bursting of the follicle, and during the twelve hours that come after it. In the days following ovulation and the death of the ovum, a woman is not able to conceive. To know when conception is possible or not, of course, can be of very great importance to a married couple when they want the birth of a child or want to postpone it.

Recent studies of female physiology have made this knowledge possible. Especially revealing is the fact that the temperature taken upon waking up in the morning is at a lower level up to the time of ovulation, then for a few days rises, and is at a higher level until about the time of the menstrual flow. This slightly higher temperature after ovulation is due to progesterone. Also, ovulation itself is nearly always accompanied by painful sensations, often slight and fleeting, or a variable pain. Before marriage, a young woman should become fully acquainted with the ways of her own individual ovarian cycle; after marriage, then, she and her husband will be much better able to live their sexual life together with full awareness and knowledge.

We say "her own individual ovarian cycle": we noted that ovulation, the bursting of the follicle, takes place twelve days more or less after the beginning of a new cycle. Actually, the time varies among individuals; one woman might detect ovulation on the eighth day, for example, while another would experience it on the seventeenth, and so on.

The age at which periods appear varies from girl to girl. However, if her periods don't appear by the time a girl is seventeen, it would be wise for her to consult a physician.

The female system when fertilization occurs. Now suppose the ovum, after breaking away from the follicle, meets with some male sex cells as it comes down through the oviduct. (How this meeting happens will be explained when we consider the facts about the man's body.)

The life of a new individual begins in the ovum as soon as it fuses with one male sex cell—a *spermatozoon.* This fertilized ovum continues on down the tube and into the uterus, where it attaches itself to the lining. If by some abnormality the ovum attaches itself in the tube, a condition results known as an *ectopic* pregnancy, which practically never comes to maturity and usually bursts the tube, creating a surgical emergency. But this occurs in only one per cent of pregnancies.

When the ovum is safely attached in the uterus, the *corpus luteum* does not wither, but increases in size and is active for several months. The muscle of the uterus remains quiet so the ovum can grow there. While

FEMALE GENITAL SYSTEM
DURING PREGNANCY

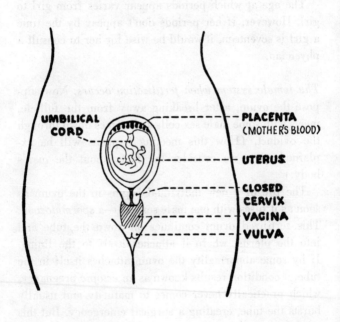

UMBILICAL CORD

PLACENTA (MOTHER'S BLOOD)

UTERUS

CLOSED CERVIX

VAGINA

VULVA

the fetus is present in the uterus no more follicles or eggs are produced. After nine months when the ovum, then called the fetus, has completed the phase of its development within the uterus it is ready to "face the outside world," that is, to be born.

Then the uterus contracts. After some hours the cervix opens, the membranes holding the fetus in a serum-like liquid break, and the child comes forth through the vagina and the vulva. This is *childbirth,* during which the mother always suffers some pain, because the uterus contracts forcibly and the genital area is stretched by the baby's head. What is called "natural childbirth" is a sort of muscular and respiratory training which a woman follows during pregnancy. The exercises are meant to make the birth more natural and more comfortable.

Before birth, the fetus was contained within the uterus, as we have seen, in a sac, and connected to a fleshy disc patch called the *placenta.* The food and oxygen that the fetus needed to live and grow came to it from the mother's bloodstream first through this placenta and then a two-channel tube (artery and vein)—the *umbilical cord.* This cord was attached to the fetus in the middle of its abdomen. After the birth of the child this cord is cut a little way from the abdomen. In a few days the cord drops off and the opening will be closed, making a scar called the *umbilicus,* or *navel.*

But the mother still has in her uterus the placenta membranes and the cord. About one half hour after the delivery, the uterus contracts once more, this time to expel these structures, called the *afterbirth*. The delivery is now completed. During the last few weeks of the pregnancy the *mammary glands* in the mother's breasts were readied to supply the *milk*, the food required by the child for its first few months of life. Now that the baby is born it can be nursed, or fed at the breast.

Throughout the pregnancy, and right up until complete delivery, there is of course no menstruation. In fact, the absence of the menstrual flow is one of the first signs that the woman is pregnant. Then, after a varying length of time following the childbirth, a period perhaps related to how long breast-feeding continues, the ovarian cycle starts again on its rhythmic activity.

When a woman nears fifty the cycle begins to stop bit by bit, and no more eggs are produced. This is the menopause, the change of life, when the menstrual flow stops entirely and the woman can no longer have children.

MAN

In men, in contrast to women, the genital organs are mostly outside the body. Also, in the outer part of their course the genital and the urinary functions are combined into a single passage. The male organs which correspond to the woman's ovaries are the *testicles.* These are contained within a skin sac called the *scrotum,* which hangs outside the abdominal cavity. In front of the scrotum hangs the *penis.*

The testicles make the male reproductive cells, the *spermatozoa.* Along the upper surface of each testicle is a passage called the *epididymis,* which leads into another passage, the *vas deferens.* Inside the abdominal cavity, under the bladder, are two organs called *seminal vesicles.* The right vas deferens merges with the outlet of the right seminal vesicle, and the left vas deferens with the outlet of the left seminal vesicle. These two combined passages, right and left, converge and go into the *prostate gland.* This passage ends in the *urethra.*

The prostate is a single gland set around the beginning of the urethral passage. The gland circles the passage as a ring circles a finger. Right next to the prostate, one above and one below, are two circular muscles. These muscles—*sphincter* muscles—can close the urethral passage tightly. The prostate itself is a very complicated gland: it behaves like an ordinary gland, giving off a slightly ropy and translucent liquid. At a certain, generally later age in a man's life, the prostate gland often becomes enlarged and interferes with the normal escape of urine through the urethra. Surgery is needed to correct this trouble, and that is why you so

MALE GENITAL SYSTEM

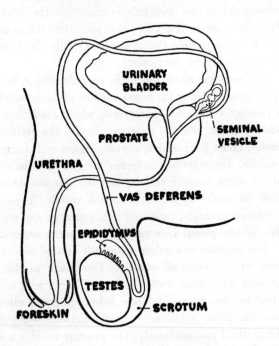

often hear that an older man has had a "prostate operation."

The penis is made up of three extended bodies set side by side. They may be thought of as large-celled sponges: when the three "sponges" are empty these organs are limp, but if blood, under pressure, of course, floods and fills these spongy bodies, the penis becomes erect, hardens, and remains this way as long as the pressure lasts. This same kind of thing—*erection*—can happen to the clitoris of the woman, although the clitoris is very much smaller than the male's penis.

Contrary to common belief, the seminal vesicles do not store up liquid the way the bladder stores up urine. As glands, they supply a liquid which will mix with the liquid from the prostate gland and carry the spermatozoa produced in the testicles. The seminal vesicles are *not* some things that "fill up, stretch, and need to be emptied from time to time," as some people think.

Normally, the testicles are always steadily producing spermatozoa, and these spermatozoa are passed out of the body through the urinary passage. The seminal vesicles and the prostate gland secrete a little liquid discharge the same way. This action is something like the salivary glands in the mouth: our saliva is constantly flowing just enough to keep the mucous membranes in our mouth moist—but we don't constantly dribble. But if we sit over a very appetizing dish, or if we're very hungry and we even think of something to eat, our saliva will overflow and we will, as they say, "start to drool" over the "mouth-watering" food.

The male sexual organ, the penis, has two different kinds of erections. The first is mostly mechanical, happening after a long night's sleep, for example, when the bladder fills and stretches and affects the sexual organ. The second kind is truly sexual. There is then some kind of *psychological* influence, either conscious or (as in sleep, for example) unconscious, causing a flow of blood to the entire genital area. The penis is distended with blood under pressure. The two sphincter muscles tighten around the urethra to block any flow of urine, and to turn the part of the urethra that runs through the prostate gland into a temporary reservoir. If sexual excitation continues, all the reflexes become exaggerated, and tension within the body mounts. Penetration of the penis into the female's vagina with rhythmic friction leads to the triggering of a climax, or orgasm. Meanwhile, spermatozoa and the liquids from the prostate gland and from the seminal vesicles accumulate fast and abundantly in the blocked-off area in the prostate gland. This mixture of fluids and spermatozoa is *semen*, which is soon let loose in a number of spurts through the urethra toward the entrance of the woman's uterus. This release—called *ejaculation*—is accompanied by a particularly intense pleasant sensation (the orgasm). The woman experiences a comparable orgasm from the stimulation of her clitoris and vagina.

Normally, the man and the woman cause each other to experience simultaneously the sensations which accompany this act, called *coitus*, or *intercourse*.

Meanwhile, the spermatozoa carried along in the sperm liquid are propelled into the woman's body against the cervix of her uterus. They enter the uterus and proceed upward as far as the oviducts. One might say they were in search of an ovum. The one which succeeds causes fertilization, but the others break down and disappear.

Now an important point: Men don't become sexually excited just because their bodies produce sperm. On the contrary, all the reflexes of genital activity, in men as in women, start from some psychological activity. The human being's desire for sexual pleasure is not like the sexual process in dumb animals; the human person's desire does not come just from the mechanical workings of the flesh.

But it's obvious that intercourse between a man and a woman is not the only possible way to cause an ejaculation and orgasm. The penis may be rubbed against something else besides just the female parts, for example. A person can play with himself, manually, to get sexually excited, and this holds true for the female (whose clitoris corresponds to the male's penis) as well as for the male. This is called *masturbation*, or self-abuse, and we'll analyze it more deeply when we discuss the psychological aspects of sexuality.

The activity of the woman's sexual organism, as we have seen, is cyclical, with the production of a new ovum once every twenty-eight days or so, from puberty to menopause. Not so with the man: he is capable of producing sperm at any time from the moment he reaches puberty and *not* stopping abruptly just when he's fifty years old or so. The ability to produce semen varies from man to man, because the formation of semen depends on how active one is sexually, and of course each man is different in this. Statistics in the United States some years ago showed that sexual activity varied from the man who might have sexual intercourse several times a day to the man who experienced only two or three "wet dreams" in a year, while asleep and possibly dreaming, a kind of unconscious masturbation.

We must conclude that everything here depends on the place that sexuality in all its forms has in the spiritual and psychological character of each individual man. It's the same for a woman; her desire to have sexual pleasure doesn't seem to be very much connected with the ovarian cycle. And if there is a connection, it's very changeable. Here again, the essential factors are psychological.

Now that we've gone over the important facts about the structure and workings of the man's and woman's reproductive systems, we'll be able to go on to take up, in the next chapter, the *psychological* aspects of sexuality.

2: SOME FACTS OF PSYCHOLOGY

2

SOME FACTS OF PSYCHOLOGY

MAN'S INSTINCT

EACH LIVING ORGANISM, whether vegetable, animal or human, is first and foremost a separate and individual set of *needs*. In fact, what makes living things basically different from dead matter like stones or water is that the existence of the living things depends on its complicated network of activities.

First comes what might be called the "need to exist." This means growing to the greatest maturity. It also means keeping at this high level of strength and intelligence by getting certain necessities (food, clothing, etc.) from the world around us. And of course it means defending this existence against any threat. All these "needs to exist" appear as drives, or instincts, which we call here *aggressive instincts*.

At the same time, each living being is itself part of a group: the *species*, or the *race*. This group, just like the individual, feels a "need to exist"; and it may even experience a real need to expand. Each living being in a group feels in its own life the needs of the group to which it belongs. This group-need has many different forms, and expresses itself in what might be called the "need to reproduce." These forms become more and more complicated as we move up the scale of living beings until we come to the higher mammals, who are the most complex of all. While the amoeba, for example, reproduces by simply splitting into two cells, the higher mammal reproduces by a very complicated coming together of two different individuals, one a male, the other a female. This need to reproduce shows itself in the *sexual instinct*.

Right now, though, we ought to point out that the two aspects of life—the individual's own need to exist, and the group's need to exist—are very, very different. The aggressive instincts are related only to the individual's single existence; this means that if these instincts are blocked the very existence of the individual is directly threatened. The sex instincts, however, are connected mainly with the group's, the species' need to exist. The sex instinct will of course *appear* in the individual members of the group, but it is serving the true needs of the species *only*. So, when the sex instincts as they appear in the individual are blocked, neither the individual's existence nor its own vital balance is directly threatened. For example, if a female animal can't mate and be fertilized, it goes on living anyway, its health in no way affected.

But there's a big difference between the world of other animals or of plants on the one hand, and the world of human beings—man—on the other. When the small animal comes to life, we can see from the very first the creature following precise, necessary patterns of behavior. The animal seems to know *in advance* just how to satisfy its needs. In the matter of sex, for example, everything generally depends upon the moment at which the female animal is able to be fertilized. When a female dog ovulates, for instance—and that happens only twice a year—a whole set of reactions follows. The bitch is said to be "in heat," and any male dog that happens around has its sex instinct stirred up. But except for this twice-a-year activity, no "extra" mating happens.

The human infant, on the contrary, is totally weak and helpless. His basic needs are the same as those of his animal counterpart, of course, and his instincts are just as strong, but the young human being, very much unlike the young animal, doesn't "know" how to apply his instinct practically. Each human individual has to *learn personally* to satisfy his needs, in a long and difficult development. This amounts to a new and special way of life: the *consciousness* of self and of one's place in the world, especially in the world of other human beings. This leaves man free to use his own will. This process of learning, this trial and error, is what each one of us goes through in order to achieve self-control. Knowledge of oneself and mastery of one's own behavior are obtained only bit by bit, in a long struggle of "live and learn," the first and early years of which remain very dim in our memory. Freudian psychology has helped enable us to understand a great deal about these shadowy but important early years in human life.

There's no reason for us to go into every stage of the psychic (mental) development of the child. Only a few landmarks must be set and explained for our understanding of sexuality.

Up until adulthood, the psychic development takes place in three major stages. The first phase comes before age seven. It is the time when the child first faces life, beginning with birth itself, and when he makes his first crude attempts to become conscious and to know about himself. In this stage the child's mind is at first mostly clouded with emotion, because clear consciousness asserts itself only gradually. After all, not many of us have a single sharp recollection of anything that happened to us when we were only six months old—and yet even then we were already ourselves.

Very early in his life the child develops what is called an "image of his body," and this is the basis of his awareness of self, the basis of his knowledge of his oneness and his separate identity, acquired little by little. There is a time, for example, when the very small child recognizes himself in a mirror and immediately turns around to the adult who is holding him—most often his mother—as if looking for confirmation that he has just discovered himself. For a long time, the only difference between boy and girl, in the child's mind, will be whether or not there is a visible sex organ. In these first phases, then, the "geography" of the body gives the child some idea of who or what he is; therefore sex is an important part of human personality from the very beginning of life.

In the course of this first stage many dramas involving the persons around him, especially his parents, unfold for the infant. Through these dramas, one after the other, the infant learns to place himself, as boy or girl, in a satisfying system of relationships with father and mother. The boiling emotions of the first seven years gradually quiet down and a kind of levelling place is reached. Psychology used to call this the "age of reason," but modern psychology now gives it the name "period of latency." This, the second stage, is a time when the various drives of instinct have just about fallen into line, the child is more or less "at ease" within himself, and he can calmly satisfy his needs for knowledge and understanding. This is the real "school age." This calm is temporary, however. It's true that the child has begun to adapt to reality by starting to control his instincts, but it's also true that his world is still a very narrow world, and that he's still very dependent on others for his food, clothes, comfort and happiness.

This "latency" stage is due to last until the beginning of adolescence. At about age thirteen—and maybe sooner for girls—a very basic change takes place, both in mind and body: that is the beginning of *puberty*, the third stage.

Physically, what happens? The body begins to take on a more adult shape; the voice changes; the chest area develops; body hairs begin to appear in certain places. This is also the time when the so-called sex organs reach their full development; the girl experiences her first menstrual flow and the boy has his first sexual arousals accompanied by the production of seminal liquid.

But the mind is more important to us, and so now we'll look more deeply into the psychological aspects of puberty and adolescence.

ADOLESCENCE

Much to his confusion, the adolescent now begins to discover that he's going to have to be involved in a world far broader than he has been accustomed to. He is led toward something new to him: personal initiative.

According to his "need to exist," taking initiative will mean more attempts to know and understand the universe which outreaches the limits of family or school. It will mean the desire for action. It will mean efforts to be recognized and accepted in the world of grownups. All this will go far to explain why, for example, an adolescent who knows very little about some particular subject will nevertheless enter endless and impassioned discussions about it. This tendency, normal though it may be, is usually annoying to adults who don't care enough to find out its significance, its subconscious meaning for the young person.

Now the "need to love" shows itself, too. The sexual instinct appears here in two different aspects: erotism—sexual desire—and sentimentality. Unlike in his early years, the adolescent now has full awareness of his sexual urges.

The onset of adolescence is usually somewhat savage. The whole balance that the child had achieved during the period of latency is now thrown into confusion. No longer a child, but not yet able to measure up to adult standards, the young person is thrown for a loop. His reactions to things are liable to be mixed, and so his actions seem contradictory.

The youth deeply desires entry into the new and wider world and is especially attracted by the idea of playing a personal part in it, but there is fear and apprehension, too, because he or she just doesn't know very much about this world. So there is an attraction and a threat at the same time, but the threat is veiled and always shifting, and even this threat, like the rest of the world, is confusing. Every vital impulse urges the young man or woman toward self-achievement, but the poor adolescent has no idea whatsoever how it will all come about. Furthermore, the fanciful and idealistic world of childhood is fast collapsing. In these difficult days it also becomes clear that familiar adults—especially one's mother and father—are not nearly as "perfect" as they had seemed; the young child had only wanted and *needed* them to be perfect. Once the adolescent understands this, of course, he will also understand that despite his imperfections it *is* possible for him to become an adult, and so he will take hope. But this transition from child's thinking to adult's thinking is always hard, no matter how good conditions are.

Sometimes the adolescent will try to escape from this awful inner struggle by turning to a world of fancy—to *dream* about life. Conversation with other people is certainly difficult for a long time, because the young person can't stand child's talk any more, but can't yet speak the way grownups do, either.

Finally, in this "leap forward" from childhood to maturity, something indefinite manifests itself, stirring the deepest and most primitive parts of the personality. Even under the best emotional conditions, a child carries away from his first years some traces of dissatisfaction, some conflicts not completely solved. None of this is really dangerous, since it may be of definite use in helping create a strong, distinct personality in the young person. But when the changes of adolescence first begin to gather speed, the youth is pulled back, without realizing it, by influences from childhood, influences which should have been outgrown. These old influences cause a vague nostalgia about childhood, and they make the growing young person reluctant to leave a childish world whose happinesses, after all, are not necessarily all in the past. Here then again is ambivalence—contradiction, vacillation—the most characteristic trait of the crisis of adolescence.

Adolescence is truly a state of crisis, with all the conditions of inner discomfort and social uneasiness. Parents usually tend, not too surprisingly, to understand and accept this, but this adjustment of theirs is always a year or two behind the actual evolution in the youngster's personality. It has to be so, because this inner evolution is dim and confusing even for the very one who is going through it.

This crisis means to the young person what the early struggles of awakening self-consciousness meant to the little child.

To understand this we'll have to look at what goes on in the very small baby. Often for some reason or other it will show a lot of discomfort. Something isn't going well with it, and nothing seems to do any good to make things better, neither a bottle to suck nor even its mother to cradle it in her arms. Then the baby discovers a way to ease the situation a little: it begins to suck its thumb, and thus in a way "escapes" into a pleasant comfortableness. What significance can we see if we think about this for a moment?

First, of course, it shows a certain weakness, that the infant isn't yet able to overcome a bad situation, and that it's completely dependent on all that surrounds it. A situation without an immediate solution plunges the baby deep into an inner sense of insecurity in which it remains even if the situation is taken care of.

Secondly, the infant's attitude is really a way of saying "I give up!" to a world in which it thinks it finds no place, no satisfaction. It locks itself in a world where there's nothing but itself. Our explanation can't, with words, give an exact idea of the baby's ways, but it can come close. The infant wants to fall back into the solitary world of self, which it does by taking, by itself and exclusively for itself, the single most concentrated source of pleasure available to it, namely the *oral* sensation (as psychologists call it), more commonly called "sucking." But sucking a thumb, of course, is only a substitute for the *true* oral pleasure, which is to suck the mother's breast (or a bottle) during the feeding period. As we older persons look at it, this pleasurableness of thumb-sucking is an empty pleasure, senseless, really useless, and without any social basis. But thumb-sucking is all the infant has for the time being.

During the following few years, the thumb-sucking tendency gradually passes away. But in moments of "big" trouble or unhappiness, the child usually returns a little to sucking his thumb. This habit may also reappear at bedtime as he drops off to sleep. When the period of latency begins, however, the habit usually disappears completely.

When the adolescent enters puberty he feels such deep inner turmoil that he once more feels the need for some self-derived, solitary pleasure. A kind of safety-valve is wanted to help release the pent-up tension, and as a result the almost-vanished feelings of his infancy come out again. Needless to say, the days of oral pleasure are long past, and, except in certain very abnormal instances, a fourteen-year-old adolescent doesn't just begin sucking his thumb again. This time, instead, the urge for self-satisfaction shifts into the area of sexual sensations.

Suddenly the young person discovers—more or less on his own—that it's possible to give oneself a very intense and mysterious sensation of pleasure. This new pleasure is strangely in tune with very old bygone emotional stirrings. This new thing is *self-abuse*, or *masturbation*. More exactly, it is self-erotic behavior, "sexual desire for oneself"; the adolescent girl's source of pleasure in this is not so much of a directly genital nature as is the boy's.

The characteristics of masturbation are basically a lot like those of thumb-sucking: the person isn't able to solve some problems in the world as it really is, so he escapes into an imaginary world filled with emotion. Both are ways of trying to experience a sensation in a void, a flight into a world where self is comfortably alone.

A *tendency* to masturbate is therefore a normal thing in an adolescent. Unlike the nursing baby's desire to suck its thumb, however, masturbation is *not* something *unavoidable*. Normally the young person should be emotionally strong enough to rise above the problem, or at least to yield to his urgings only once in a while.

We have to look at the details here. Every serious statistical study that we have shows clearly that under the present conditions in our society at least ninety-five per cent of boys and young men between thirteen and twenty-five years of age pass through periods of *habitual* masturbation of varying lengths. Varying conditions in home or school don't seem to make much difference. These periods of masturbation may be only a few months, or many years. In girls, as we've already suggested, the problem is different, because although only forty to fifty per cent are found to actually masturbate (with the genital parts), their self-excitation does take other forms, such as caressing the body, having sentimental thrills, "crushes," and so on.

These are the hard facts. But we have to try to understand these facts. Masturbation may happen often, but we can't just conclude that it's normal. The "common cold," for example, may be common, but it certainly isn't normal; it's a sickness all the same. Frequency does not prove normality, nor does rarity necessarily mean abnormality. Modern psychology has been making it more and more clear that there are several good reasons why the adolescent rarely goes through puberty without falling at least once into the habit of masturbation: (1) the lack of frank and clear sex education during childhood, (2) the notion—which is still as strong as ever—that sex is not to be talked about openly, and (3) the stern and overly moral educational policies often found in schools and other institutions. These things are all the more troublesome precisely because the *tendency* toward erotic self-excitation (*not* the masturbation itself) is normal. This all means that if the necessary safeguards were given to the adolescent, he would be able to avoid falling into the habit of masturbation.

Just what is wrong with masturbation? We should understand this clearly and definitely, because too often people either go overboard about the horrible results of the habit or else simply deny that there is *anything* wrong with it.

Some people, having read certain old-fashioned books about "morality" or medicine, go around spreading ignorance and misinformation on the subject. If we listen to them we get the idea that habitual masturbation will bring on sterility, tuberculosis, insanity, and various other catastrophes. All of this is not true, yet now and then this kind of nonsense, in one form or another, is widely believed.

Masturbation has practically no physical consequences, either for good or for bad. If it is extremely frequent—as where it is a frenzy, a symptom of mental illness—then it may have some echoes in the overall physical being. But this is true only in very bad cases where all sorts of things might be causing the physical troubles. The over-simplified trick of telling an adolescent that he's ruining his health when he masturbates is not only foolishness, but a lie. It only complicates an already difficult problem, first by mixing falsehood with everyone's worries on the matter, and second by making the adolescent doubt everything else he might have been told.

The real drawbacks of habitual masturbation do exist, and they are of a psychological kind. The basic drawback is that it stops the normal personality development of the child into a man, it retards the emotional coming-of-age. Roughly speaking, so long as the habit persists, the youth is not ready to come into his full powers; his instinctive attempt to escape reality continues. Masturbation isn't exactly the cause of this attitude, but it certainly complicates things. And if the young person becomes more and more worried about this, his insecurity will increase and it will be even more difficult for him to break out of the habit.

Now, the sexual instinct has two main and rather separate parts: *erotism,* or the passionate desire for sexual pleasure, is the sensuous part, while *tender feeling* is the affectionate, emotional part. During the crisis of adolescence these two parts haven't yet been brought into harmony with each other. There may even be moments of considerable wavering, as when a boy has feelings of amorous tenderness for another younger boy, while at the same time indulging in masturbation inspired by fancies of female forms. As long as the masturbation lasts and serves as a sort of way of "meeting" reality, those two parts, sensuality and tenderness, cannot blend in harmony.

Let's look at how these things work out in the case of a "normal" boy of today, normal in the sense that he's not sick, not morbid, not abnormal.

Johnny is fourteen. On his own, or with the instruction of a pal, he discovers masturbation. Let's assume he has nothing to help him understand what is happening, no good advice, no way of measuring the right and wrong, the good and bad in these new matters. At most he has a vague notion that it is something that "you just don't do," and so he instinctively hides away as he does it. The habit takes hold. Only after a while does Johnny become aware that this is a problem, and a "moral" problem to boot. But he doesn't have any very clear notions about that, unless they are false ones gotten from friends. The problem as he sees it is distorted by a mysterious feeling of guilt.

At first the fancies that excite his imagination are vague: feminine forms in blurred confusion, nameless and faceless. But pretty soon the daydreams come into clearer focus, picturing real women he knows, particularly the pin-up girls of lewd magazines. Johnny begins to buy such magazines, through which he gets to "know" a woman in only two dimensions, the photograph. This is the normal tendency of a fourteen- to sixteen-year-old boy (and this is true of a few fiftyish "old boys" who have a fondness for the same photographic fare).

Soon, though, Johnny begins to feel a hollow sense of dissatisfaction touched with bitterness. As his instinctive worry in the face of the mystery of the female world grows less, as it certainly will if he makes the effort to know and get along with girls, he begins to think of sexual relations with a "three-dimensional" woman, a real woman. This doesn't mean that Johnny is ready to live with a woman yet, but it at least shows that he has desire for an *object* that has greater reality, more substance than the figures in his solitary dream-life.

He can satisfy his yearnings in either of two ways. First, he may resort to a woman who sells her body, the prostitute. In that case, the human relationship is just about zero. Moreover, since John is a normal boy, he'll in fact be more disappointed than he will ever admit to anyone. The use of a prostitute is basically so little different from self-abuse that it is definitely not even a beginning to the solution of the problem of masturbation.

John's other choice is the so-called easy woman, who allows herself to be sweet-talked, and is taken to bed with very little trouble. However old she may be physically, her mental age is the same as Johnny's so far as development of her personality goes. But here, after all, there is at least a new dimension, the hint of a human relationship, however thin it may be. In fact, however, it remains for both of them a backing away from a genuine human commitment. This "affair" is still sexual *self*-satisfaction (auto-erotism) and a psychological turning back into oneself (egocentrism). It is a pursuit of emotional and sensuous satisfaction by each partner's using the other chiefly as a tool. Even if Johnny himself falls for the illusion that he is in love, the woman is still really just a thing to him. He's not yet able to take into account her personal mystery, nor to commit himself to her as one living, imperfect being to another, for a *life* together. And if Johnny should give up all efforts at moral thought, and let these intimacies extend into a lengthy affair, he wouldn't be proving his manliness, even though he might think so, so much as he would be proving that he's almost unable to emerge from adolescence.

Now let's assume that John, who has been taught "high principles" but who hasn't been shown a real sense of spiritual values, nor any of the essential facts of sex, begins to throw off all religious practice because of his affair. He'll masturbate less and less now, but will take up sexual relations with various girl friends. He is now nineteen. On day he meets a new girl—Jane. She is eighteen, charming, and of course physically attractive to him. But all these details somehow seem to stay in the background. The fact is that he finds his chief interest in Jane in something else besides beauty. He wants to know what she thinks, he wants to discuss a certain book, a film, a problem with her. He wants to know her way of looking at things so that he can revise his own opinions. In brief, he shows signs of wanting to establish with her a relationship of mutual exchange which little by little shows signs of becoming permanent. Life now will have its full meaning for John only in a constant dialogue with *her*.

This experience is new to John, and it calls into question all his previous ideas of womanhood and of life itself. He begins to believe in love again, after all his thoughtless adventures with easy women, but this time it's a romantic love. He doesn't *at first* really want to have sexual relations with Jane. And if he does think of having intercourse with her, the desire doesn't show itself as immediate and irrepressible lust, but appears to him instead as the end point of a deep and lasting relation. He finds himself surprised to be thinking of sexual intercourse as the meeting of two people who will eventually produce a third human being. To his eyes, now, Jane appears destined to become not only his personal companion, but also the mother of his children.

John's transformation runs deep, much to his own amazement. Without his notice, and without any effort on his part, all traces of the old adolescent masturbation habit, whether solitary or with a chance partner, begin to disappear. Soon John finds himself master of his sexual urges, not mastered by them any more; he knows now his capacity for love, not for just any attractive girl, but for *one person*—his chosen partner.

At this moment, then, John has reached a stage of emotional maturity that is quite difficult to attain. Now an adult, fully grown mentally and physically, he is able to practice sexual self-restraint. In him the two separate parts of the sex instinct, the erotic and the emotional, draw together and become a harmonious one.

We must understand, though, that this development of the personality is only a part of a whole growing process, and is not reducible to the sex aspect alone. In the course of these few years of his life John has gone on with his schooling, or he has been working at a job. He has had social contact with all sorts of people. He has gradually learned to act positively in the world, and has governed his own life. In short, he has adjusted normally to human society and found his place in it. His personality has grown to its full and true limits. He has a measure of self-assurance. John has by now met and overcome some failures, has come to make the most of good opportunities, and has left behind his old dreams in order to pledge his energies to the real, and to the expected future. His imagination is no longer the escape route from reality that it used to be, but has become the gateway to ever increasing creativeness.

Obviously this little story of John's evolution doesn't include all the possibilities. We told the story the way it happens in most cases, and we deliberately played down any abnormal tendencies. We ought to look now at a few of the special problems.

Remember that John's early female sex partners, as we saw in the story of his adolescence, were treated by him as *things* rather than as *persons*. But it is a fact that sexuality involves far greater personal commitments than does any other kind of encounter between human beings. First of all, this is because of its intenseness, but also because it is a biological function which potentially means the appearance of a third human being, the child. In one way of looking at it, then, sexual intercourse between a man and a woman who don't commit themselves permanently to one another is really a subhuman act.

Such excursions into sexual relations may not leave too deep a mark upon the boy, but this is certainly not true for the girl. Here is another fact: the stirring up of sexuality, in either its erotic or its emotional sense, leaves far deeper and wider marks on the girl's personality than on the boy's. She may be hurt permanently or even thrown out of adjustment by these irresponsible adventures. She will fall into an insecurity which is made all the worse by the fact that it is an unconscious insecurity, one which she'll try to avoid facing up to. The boy, on the other hand, can break away with a very selfish nonchalance. Yet even the boy doesn't really get off scot free, because something else enters the picture here.

During the adolescent crisis some reactions become obsessions, and occur again and again. The habit of self-abuse may easily become this kind of unpleasant obsession. In fact, for some time a boy is usually really dependent on masturbation, and can't break the habit even if he wants to. A sort of mental compulsion takes hold of him. This young fellow doesn't understand what the obsession means, so, without looking into it more deeply, he just calls it a "physical thing," thus proving again how widespread the false notions about the physiological aspects of male sexuality are. When adolescence nears its end, masturbation usually disappears, or else is replaced by sexual relations with partners of the opposite sex. Certainly the boy's sexual behavior has changed, because he no longer goes in for "solitary" pleasures, but his reactions to his new-style sex activity still bear the stamp of the old habit of masturbation. This old habit may not reappear consciously, but will persist as a subconscious pattern. In this way, intercourse with a woman may be nothing more than disguised masturbation. This is one of the usually unheeded drawbacks to those premarital "experiences" that are, without exaggeration, just about as bad a preparation for married life as are outright ignorance or inhibition. These "trial marriage" experiments are confusing demonstrations of doubts and fears.

But the main point is this: for the young man who shortly before was strongly addicted to masturbation, sexual relations with his wife won't be much different from his previous acts of masturbation. He won't realize this, he certainly won't want it to be so, and his real love for his wife (there must be some, of course) will go to contradict this tendency; but usually nothing is done about the situation. He's so used to the self-centered pleasures of masturbation that he can't help it when these old ways keep going even in his new life. Pretty soon he'll just be releasing his *own* sensuous urges on his wife, without being able to take into account his wife's different feelings, the special wants that *she* has. This strange kind of "off-center" intercourse is very frequent among newlyweds; it prevents the harmonizing of sexual relations that they so eagerly want. Yet, if we think over the startling figures about the commonness of masturbation that we looked at earlier, we shouldn't be too surprised about these later problems. It's sad but true that a thing like this can nearly ruin the life of a married couple. If this part of the foundations of marriage goes unrepaired, misunderstanding may slowly seep through and destroy the attention that the husband gives (or should give) to the wife.

The man is sometimes mislead by his enjoyment of sexual intercourse into thinking that his *psychological* liking for masturbation has been entirely corrected. Without his knowing it, though, the old habit may have left in him a hidden layer of leftover adolescent thinking. If he happens to be separated from his wife for a long time for some reason or other, or if he otherwise has to stop having intercourse with her, the husband may find, to his great annoyance, that he starts masturbating again as he used to in his teens. This lack of control over the sexual urges is also one of the things that causes difficulties when the couple are trying to space out the births of their children.

Johnny's development is obviously far from ideal. There are too many psychological problems in him which are only covered over rather than solved.

The ideal would be when the boy gradually gets positive instruction about sex, and when his questions about sex are given straight answers. His family life should let him grow without too much conflict, and should be a real help to him in the inevitable unrest of his adolescent crisis. Forewarned is forearmed, and when the tendency toward masturbation first appears he would be able to understand the meaning of the first few accidental masturbations and would *not* sink into the habit. Instead of drifting aimlessly in confusion and anxiety, he would be able to see a clear way through the crisis. Hidden complications (especially the habit of masturbation) would be kept at a minimum. He would be able to reach young adulthood much more quickly, balancing his personality and showing self-assurance. Everyone can see the difference between these two boys, the one self-confident and responsible, the other unable to show strength of character, unable to control the various powers within himself.

3: THE YOUNG GIRL GROWS UP

3

THE YOUNG GIRL GROWS UP

PUBERTY BEGINS FOR THE GIRL when she has her first menses. This is the sign that she's soon going to run into important problems.

Most adolescent girls are deeply affected by the first menstrual flow. They eagerly want it to come, but at the same time they're displeased by it. It's disturbing in many ways, because it's a change in the body and because it's a break with the carefree world of childhood.

The monthly occurrence has a whole chain of consequences, but the girl usually notices only the unpleasant ones: abdominal pains, general nervous tension, ill-temper, anxiety. Her brothers and friends all say, "She's having her period—let's leave her alone," really meaning "She'll be O.K. again in a few days."

And it *is* true that for the three or four days when she has her "period" the young lady has changing moods, from black pessimism to high good spirits, often making great drama out of tiny incidents which would ordinarily go unnoticed.

Little by little her attitudes toward the family change, particularly toward mother, against whom a kind of irritation begins to simmer. She would like her mother to be aware of her new evolution, because deep down, although she might not admit it, she's proud of it. But at one and the same time she doesn't want her mother to know about it at all, either. Modesty and shame make her want to hide it, but it really does give her an inner glow. Feeling that nobody, not even her family, understands her, she becames generally dissatisfied and pulls back into her own shell. She becomes more and more secretive, cutting herself off from her parents. She's quite content to give them the impression that she's a stranger in their midst, a close-lipped visitor whose real thoughts are confided only to a carefully guarded "Dear Diary."

Carol dimly feels the stirring of desires within herself, desires that amaze her. Her changing body arouses her own interest, and she begins to notice the glances of those around her, of her parents and relatives, but particularly of the boys. All these people are evidently beginning to consider her as a "someone."

In the past, as a "little" girl, she may have experienced certain sensations of pleasure in her genital parts, and she may even have developed the habit of rubbing herself there as she was falling asleep, for example, but it was only an unconscious, unknowing act. Now she *consciously* discovers that some parts of her body—the clitoris, the breasts—are a source of possible pleasure. But still, girls don't fall into the habit of masturbation as much as boys do. Pleasure can come to the girl in many other ways, because her *whole* body is now aroused and sensitive, not just one part of it as with the boy. Every part of her body becomes sensitive to touches, caresses, kisses, and she seeks all of these for sensuous pleasure. Carol's whole body pleases her, and she wants to adorn it. She becomes a flirt, giving every little part of her body long and careful attention. She neglects nothing that she thinks can make her more attractive, spending a lot of time with the set of a hair-do, the curve of an eyebrow, the shape and coloring of a fingernail.

As she becomes more coquettish this way, she begins to hate any physical exertion as a possible threat to the perfection of her model-like beauty. The boys now see her as stuck-up, worried only about scratches and cuts, afraid to peel potatoes, in dread of getting dishpan hands. But she doesn't even want to eat potatoes—or any other high-calorie, fattening food. She wants always to be seen only at her best. She especially likes dancing, for example, because there she feels many pleasures at once: "digging" the music, blending her movements with a partner in one rhythm, and embracing him. This is her first flight into freedom.

Carol knows that all these new interests are more or less connected with sex in some way. What then does she think of them?

Her reactions are contradictory: there is pleasure, of course, but she also has doubts about them. They seem to be dangers somehow. She has several possible ways of dealing with this upsurge of sex instinct.

First, she might try to refuse to satisfy her natural wants—this is called *asceticism*. She'll try to think of eating, sleeping, and love of ease as "lower instincts," and she'll think of people who enjoy those things as "uncouth" or "low class." She may also go overboard trying to become as slender as possible, showing a horror of the well-rounded female form that may even inspire her almost to refuse to eat at all. This last can easily become a serious illness called "mental anorexia," a dangerous loss of appetite which will have a bad effect on the whole body both physically and mentally. But let's assume that Carol doesn't go that far. We find that she'll live through her period of asceticism with strange interruptions during which she'll shake free of it with a vengeance, and indulge her natural needs in sudden spurts of party-going, shopping, or stuffing herself with candy.

This strange behavior is just another demonstration of the conflicting values of adolescence: attraction-repulsion, desire-fear. The girl teeters between on one side the desire to give in to her instincts (especially the sexual instincts) and, on the other, disgust for this femininity which makes life so difficult for her. The ascetic phase of some adolescent girls is like this, and the boys simply cannot see any sense in the girl's actions. They only shrug their shoulders and complain that "girls are as changeable as the weather . . . too complicated . . . don't ever trust them."

Carol's second way of reacting to these slightly dangerous instincts is to intellectualize them. Like the boys, she may develop a taste for juggling ideas, then become obsessed with abstract thinking, and so be able to turn the new desires which threaten her balance into milder, abstracted speculations. In the unending search for the balance that concerns them so much—though they usually don't admit it—boy and girl adolescents often seem to find some kind of reassurance in thinking over the great problems which are the same for them as for their predecessors of previous generations. This whole process is normal and well suited to the crisis through which they're living now, but as an obsession it must be outgrown as adulthood approaches.

Unfortunately, some adolescent girls never outgrow

this stage. They can't resist turning everything into ideas, and they eventually become so caught up by this that they make it into their way of life, a way that will quite shrivel them up. They try hard to get rid of all their sensitiveness, intuition, charm, tenderness and daintiness, seeing them as flaws in the female sex, flaws opposed to "reason." Many young women rightly aiming at intellectual careers become entirely de-feminized; they remind us of modern versions of some women university graduates of twenty years ago or so, who made a big point of not knowing how to darn a sock or cook an egg, as if there were only one clear-cut choice: to be intellectuals, or to be just plain, common women.

Finally, still other girls try to settle the problem of awakening sexual instinct by fencing these instincts in within a rigid set of principles made up for their own private use. These are really not principles, but rather just personal quirks, any violation of which is considered intolerable by the girl. In this third type of escapism, a girl sees her oncoming womanhood as a tidal wave, against which she has to build a firm dike of "principles." These principles express themselves often as ritualistic and excessive cleanliness, for example, or odd finicky ways followed as closely and carefully as though they were true rules of spiritual life.

The girl's social attitudes develop in ways very similar to the boy's.

We saw that Carol has drawn away from family life, even though she's still actually in the midst of the family. She acts aloof and independent, but this pose bothers her quite a bit. Wobbling between the urge to retire within herself and the excitement of the outside world, she looks around for a workable solution. Her search leads her to idealistic friendships, to intense, exclusive attachments to girl friends or adult women, with guarantees of her "absolute, everlasting faithfulness" to them. She has mad crushes for a teacher, an adviser, some famous woman, a "star" maybe, to whom she feels close for some reason. She will adopt this other woman's ideas, manners, dress. All this is only for a time, though, and disappointment comes fast.

Jealous, tight friendships are more common among young girls than among young boys, and they might just be a way of escaping the seeming danger of attraction toward the male sex. Boys are *forbidden* to enter here! Society approves of friendship between young people of the same sex, and so nothing stands in the way of such a "friendship" becoming so passionate that one of the two girls will suddenly realize that things have gone too far, feel guilty, and finally become frightened and break away. And yet in fact their relationship as friends was real and deep; if only other people had been allowed to enter and share in it it might have been beautiful and lasting.

This kind of jealous friendship might take another

shape. Girls often band together in groups, in little cliques which crowd out any friendships with boys. Outwardly seeming to be at their ease, protected, the girls let themselves be confined within such small clubs. Boys, of course, look at these closed circles as more or less hostile groups which they don't dare approach. The girls, really prisoners of the all-female social circle, are made to feel that any interest in boys would be treason. More than that, the group considers even an engagement to be married as a betrayal rather than as the desirable and normal thing that it actually is.

It's not uncommon for a very young girl to carry the torch for a boy her own age. At fifteen or sixteen, a girl often decides that she wants to find a boy who, though not exactly her fiancé, will be hers alone, her escort to parties, her "steady." She doesn't realize, of course, that this desire is entirely self-centered, to satisfy her wish to be looked at and admired. She does need someone, yes, but only someone to hold the mirror so she can look at herself.

The young girl is right in the middle of all her adolescent problems, deeply upset by the awakening of her sexuality—so she's not yet really capable of true love, which requires giving as well as receiving.

The young man at this age or even a few years older is also seldom ready for a lasting love relationship. And so things happen which he later regrets, sad adventures like the following.

Ann is bored and lonely. The telephone is handy. She calls Jimmy, whom she met just a few days ago. They talk, and then, because neither one of them has anything better to do, they agree to meet in a half-hour. Ann is now excited by the prospect of a nice afternoon. In the few minutes left before her date arrives she pretties herself up, and when Jimmy comes in he gets a warm greeting. Ann has found someone to please, an admirer. Unconsciously she becomes flirty. Jimmy, on his part, naturally expects at first only that he and she are going to be just friends, without any fuss or serious attentions. Soon, however, something about the way Ann is acting strikes him as being a bit seductive. From there it is only a short step to Jimmy's becoming sexually excited. But this isn't the way Ann had honestly expected the date to turn out. Baffled and even a little indignant at the boy's reactions, she makes some attempts to defend herself, but sooner or later she gives in and, not thinking of the tremendous consequences, agrees to sexual intercourse. When in due time she realizes that she's pregnant everything becomes a catastrophe. Ann will have to have a face-saving marriage to please morality, family and society. Thus a hasty "home and family," really unwanted by both parties, comes into being—born of an ill-timed and thoughtless casual relationship.

Ann and Jim will live with bitterness and disappointment in the months following their wedding. Their union is a mismatch because it wasn't prepared for by long mutual acquaintance and social exchange. Neither is long satisfied; in disgust, and ruing the loss of her freedom, Ann wants a divorce, while Jim admits his mistake.

Things don't always happen just this way, of course. Whereas Ann gave in to Jimmy's lust out of weakness or lack of understanding of what she was doing, many other girls would have drawn back in anger and offense at the young man's conduct. They would consider him odious, repulsive. They wouldn't be at all conscious of the fact that it was they themselves who led him into temptation. From there the false equation comes too easily to them: all boys are disgusting!

In either case, neither party understands the other's reactions. Jimmy saw sexual desire and seduction in what was on Ann's part merely a flirtation, a desire to be admired. And Ann, herself not aware of the force of male reactions, is at fault for provoking the unforeseen sexual impulse which flared out of control more violently than she expected. She was only teasing, that is true, but Jim responded to what he felt as a demand for the complete sexual act.

The male sex urge is intense, concentrated and very easily triggered indeed. Its release mechanism can be set off without any preparation of affection or love.

Bodily contacts alone can do it for the boy, and so can those "innocent" little kisses which a girl thinks she can give without trouble because it's "the thing to do," and rather pleasant.

When these things are done casually, a man's sexual desire is quickly aroused, quickly satisfied, and just as quickly drained away. But not for the woman. Haste leaves her upset and unsatisfied. She is able to have a satisfying sexual relationship *only* after a long mental and physical preparation. This preparation determines the quality of the love relationship. Intercourse satisfies her only as a high point of her closeness to the man in other parts of their life together.

So a woman's sex instinct is stirred up much more slowly than a man's in spite of how much she may flirt. Therefore she may resent man's sex drive as something brutal and unpleasant *unless* it's just one part of a deep relationship. But even then this relationship has to be more than a slap-bang affair that lacks a long physical and emotional preparation.

Now, the man, as we said, can satisfy his sex desire quickly and somewhat mechanically, but still and all he will have the most satisfying orgasm only when the sexual relationship is harmonious. And "harmonious" means when he can feel that the woman deeply shares his satisfaction. There will be no joy for the one without joy for the partner, too. There must be a mutual "gift," where each stops just taking and begins giving of the self to the other.

In a couple's life together, love must be continually created. It doesn't simply appear at the beginning and last throughout the marriage. Love must be studied and learned, in a way, on all levels. Along with a strong emotional, intellectual and spiritual fellowship there comes a slow maturing, a time when the sexual gift quietly seeps inward. Early sexual relations, with their self-centeredness and their emphasis on self-satisfaction, give no hint of this later, greater happiness.

Looked at this way, sexual life no longer seems like a delightful toy, nor even as a mere portion of married life. It truly blends into the whole marriage so completely as to become the very symbol of the couple's happy life together. This is certainly a far cry from the cheap excitements of "quickie" affairs. This greater joy is the true "genital" love, the companionship of two people whose sexual exchanges are really a kind of translation of the total love they feel for each other.

4: GOD'S WORD

4

GOD'S WORD

NEVER BEFORE HAS SO MUCH LIGHT been thrown on the subject of sexuality as today, with the researches of modern science. But scientific understanding is not enough.

It is fairly easy to see ways in which a person's personality can be made better, but we have to realize that this can never go as far as final perfection. Better, yes; perfect, no. The absolutely perfect human being doesn't exist. Everyone has times when he instinctively draws back within himself, to zones "off limits" to other people. We are never, in our relations—including sexual relations—ever completely open with each other.

Even the existence of sexuality itself is a great contradiction. Sex is obviously a basic source of personality differences; men have personalities basically very different from women's. But sexual love itself—the physical act of intercourse—is *not* an absolute necessity. This means that a human being is really an individual personality only if the person, if a male, acts like a man, and if a female, acts like a woman. Despite the fact that a person needs to have a sex, the person may very well do without "genital" sexual relations of any kind. Let's call being male (or female) and behaving like a man (or woman) *sexed;* and let's think of sex love, physical or emotional, as *sexual.*

Finally, even physical and emotional sexual love itself contains contradictions. The sexual urges and emotions are strong and intense, but they only last for a very short time. Because of this great intensity and extreme briefness sexual intercourse has been called "an illusion of infinity." Also, the sexual act doesn't make up the whole meaning of love any more than the "genital" part of life makes up the whole life of a human couple.

If we want to know more about all this, then, we'll have to get our understanding from somewhere else than from modern science alone. Our *own* discoveries and self-contemplations can't tell us everything about ourselves. We have to find out what someone other than

ourselves, someone above our human limitations, has to
say. We must hear what God himself tells us about the
mystery of ourselves.

Revelation in the Holy Scriptures helps us penetrate
the mystery of our sexuality. It is our nature as human
beings to live and act to the best of our conscious abili-
ties in all things, so it follows that we must know as
much about sex as we can. And a morality not based
upon the word of God would be as unhuman as a
morality that would deny today's scientific knowledge
of human realities.

The first two chapters of Genesis show—symbolically
—what really happened at the creation of the world
and the human race. And symbolic it has to be, because
we just don't have facts about the earliest days of the
world the way we do about the most recent five or six
thousand years in history. Genesis records the very beginnings of human history, beginnings which for scientific investigation are lost in a haze. Divine revelation
casts a light on these beginnings and sets their real
meaning in clear outline.

According to both of these chapters, it is Man *and*
Woman who inseparably make up the human race. This
doesn't say anything about the worth of *each individual*
human person, nor about the spiritual image of God in
the world, but just that Man and Woman together make
humanity. This is as God intends it, so that he can

make himself closer to mankind. The first story of Genesis, in Chapter 1, even tells that the male and the female were created at one and the same time.

More than that: the image of God according to which mankind was created *demands* that there be both male and female. "And God created man to his own image: to the image of God he created him: male and female he created *them*." At first this is amazing. To think of God as having sex seems absurd, a return to the wild fancies of mythology. But let's think a little about it: to be in the image of God, the human race at its beginning must have been made up of two *persons*, different and alike at the same time, each one pushed toward the other by the drive of love in such a way that from their unity there shall come forth a possible "third person": the child.

There is a parallel here, strange as it may seem, between Revelation and modern psychology. According to psychology, a human being reaches the necessary fullness of personality only by being able to adjust himself to a "triangular situation." This is the stage in emotional development that Freud called the "Oedipus crisis." It is the period when the child, as *boy* or *girl*, forms a relation with the parents as they are a couple, instead of as before when the child tended to feel closer to one parent than to the other. The married couple, on the other hand, achieves its own fullest life only if it is fertile and is the fountainhead from which comes a child, the "third person." This is the "triangular situation."

Following such thoughts, the image of God in mankind can be seen as the relationship between *persons*, especially among *three* persons. As for God himself, we know from the full revelation of the Holy Spirit that in his basic essence God is the Mystery of the *Trinity*.

Still another aspect of sexuality comes to light as Revelation further unfolds. This other aspect is a basic theme in the Bible, starting nine centuries before the birth of Christ with the words of the prophet Osee, resumed in fine detail by Ezechiel (Chapter 16) and found throughout the entire Canticle of Canticles of Solomon. This theme is the love of the spouse for the bride. This is the one comparison that can give us some insight into the mystery of what goes on between God and mankind. It tells us that the love of man for woman has meaning of and by itself, aside from the importance of potential childbearing. Expressing such a love through the sexual act is only one aspect of the love, of course, but still it really *is* that love, although a translation of it, so to speak. Therefore we come to a very simple conclusion: when sexual intercourse really expresses the mutual love of the man and woman, it cannot help being in line with God's call, and therefore good; but if the sexual act is not an expression of such love, it is destructive and evil.

This is what gives marriage its meaning as a *sacra-*

ment. Human love, intended by God to be the point wherein man resembles him, became after the coming of Christ a real *sign* of his Presence and, also, a way for man to become more like God. Even if a man and woman marry after her menopause, with no chance of their having children, their marriage is completely valid in the eyes of the Church on one condition: that neither one of them be impotent. In other words, they must still be able to carry on sexual relations.

When we look at things in this way, we can get a better understanding of the meaning of "Christian" marriage. Contrary to what too many people believe, the Christian idea of a married couple doesn't run against natural sex desires. Far from it: the Christian concept accepts these urges, and only wants to help them to their full meaning.

Perhaps we'd better strongly underline one thing that doesn't always come right to mind: reproductive sexuality, when it is once set in motion, has a definite social importance. This means that it goes beyond the couple itself and becomes the concern of the couple's social surroundings and, ultimately, the concern of the world. If a man and a woman exchange kisses, they alone are involved. But if they have intercourse, becoming one, they create at least the possibility of a third person: a child. At the moment of intercourse, a whole new world of relationships and responsibilities comes into existence. The child, in order to become a good, balanced human being itself, will need in its emotional life a security and stability which the mother alone can give. The mother herself, in turn, needs the sense of security that will come to her only through being close to the child's father. And all of this depends, finally, on the strong and proper organization of the social environment that surrounds them. We know that in all kinds of human society the married couple need the "consent" of their social group in order to be truly happily married. The way in which this consent is given by the group is different from society to society, but everywhere the idea of "marriage" boils down to just this consent of the group.

Now we come to this: there are two *basic* kinds of society. First there are "natural" societies, societies seen in place and in time (history). These natural societies are the family, tribe, nation, group of nations, and so forth. The other kind is the Society called the Church or the *Ecclesia* (its Greek name). "Ecclesia" means "assembly"; it doesn't change from place to place or time to time. It rises above all time limits. It is of all men of all times of all places. It is the assembly of men resurrected in and with Christ. No one name can fully define this ultimate community of human destiny, but the different possible names do cast some light on its essential aspects: Church, Ecclesia, Kingdom of Heaven, Mystical Body. This supreme society, however, exists in earthly time, and has its roots here below. Marriage then becomes this supreme society's way of recognizing the couple in the making. And it is here, at this level, that the mutual pledging of man to woman and woman to man becomes a *sacrament*.

The word "sacrament" is such a commonly used word that we'll have to try a special way of getting to understand it. A brief story may help us. A husband comes home at the end of the day. As soon as he opens the door to his house he perceives many things. There are noises coming from the kitchen; the smell of food cooking is in the air; his wife's coat is on a hanger in the hallway; the children's books and school bags are scattered around; there are voices, footsteps, a general hubbub. All these things tell the husband that there is someone here now, someone he doesn't yet see. But this is obviously not just anyone there for no particular reason but his *wife* who is there for *him*. And he has come home for *her*.

What then is a sacrament? It is the unquestionable sign of the real presence of someone we don't see, but who is nevertheless there in the greatness of his Presence: the risen Christ. Marriage is indeed a sacrament; the promising of the couple one to the other, and the relationship of love which joins these two human beings for the full length of their existences, these become at once the signs of the very real presence of the living God. Christ takes this mutual "I do" and makes it an irreplaceable moment in the Covenant he has pledged with all humanity.

This is what gives married life a dimension of infinity.

In Genesis the love of the spouses for each other is shown to be an important step toward the understanding and the wholeness that is the foundation of this world. Now something is added to this. In Christ this love, although set in the here and now of the earth, is also really the first step in the construction of the Kingdom of Heaven. The sexual—meaning genital—expression of their love will be transcended in the world of the Resurrection, but their life as a couple is still the foreshadowing, the seed of the risen, finest world.

Their love is fertile, too, and that means that God has entrusted to human love the power to work with him in the creation of that finest humanity. Not only are the man and wife a small likeness of the love relationship in eternity, but they are also actually building the Ecclesia, the Church, by adding their children to it as new members. These children are indeed "living stones," as Saint Peter describes them.

In giving us other signs of his presence, Christ used symbols—water, bread, wine—along with his words. For the marriage sacrament though, he accepts the words by themselves, the "I do" uttered by each partner in agreement to their mutual call. No other symbol is needed. But this much is clear: that there is no true sacrament here unless the pledge is between person and person, a commitment in which each acknowledges the other as a *subject*, not as an *object* of possession. Together they are the couple, they are one, and this is for all time. In the Christian view the word "divorce" has no meaning. Either marriage is for life, or there is no marriage. If there is a real marriage, then nothing in this world can "put asunder" what God "hath joined together."

Pledged to married life this way, the man and the woman partake in what is truly a "vocation." God "calls" each one through the other's voice, and calls both together as one to what Saint Paul tells us is "the adoption in Christ." This is a pooling of existences in the highest sense. It is not some vague mingling of dream personalities sunk into some abstract namelessness; quite to the contrary. It is a set of living relationships in which each individual has to accentuate his individuality, becoming more and more truly himself through his actions toward others and toward God. Two people in marriage can't have exactly the same *inner* experiences, for not everything can be expressed, nor can every little thing be shared. But they must make continuous efforts to be in agreement about all evident things, to hit it off with each other in every way possible. That is how earthly happiness, relatively speaking, will come about for two people in day-to-day living. This happiness is the immediate test of the spiritual quality of their union. The presence of Christ shows up in the *realities* of daily life. A couple who might try to become "spiritually one" while giving no thought to providing enough food for themselves every day would be living in the clouds of a pious but unfortunate delusion.

The period of engagement before marriage has an important connection with all that has just been said. The engagement unfolds, usually, in two stages. First, having met (in the sense of true love mutually discovered), the young man and the girl—really, in a way, secretly engaged—learn to know each other better and to overcome personal selfishness. For each of them this stage is the beginning of the cutting of ties with the past, this past that brought them where they are.

The second stage is reached when the social group gives its consent and accepts the fact that these two people have really and finally decided to come together. This second is the formal, official engagement, and it should never run for too long a time. This is because it is a time when the two young people will definitely tend toward sexual union, and so the engagement can't be allowed to last indefinitely without serious trouble.

As a strong preparation for a whole life of togetherness, the engagement time ought to be the period during which the young man and his fiancée face up together to all the problems that they think they're going to have, start creating mutual understanding, and begin the entire foundation of the marriage they are about to start building, with death the only stopping point. We would best like to see these young people, in the beginnings of their love, think thirty years or so into the future, to the days when their children will set out on their own separate careers. With these future events in mind, we would like to see them plan now about how they're going to find each other again at that future time, when they'll be alone together again. That far-off time of the declining years will be the most serene and delicately tender years if they have known how to prepare for them.

Chapter 3 of Genesis, in the same style used in Chapters 1 and 2, tells the story of what is traditionally known as "the Fall," or "Original Sin."

Once again we must take this story as symbolically rather than literally true; what we read in this chapter is not a flat "news report" or so-called true story that "actually happened." The Bible narrative here is only an *allegory*, with the facts presented as a story, but it does present a profound historical fact: the real encounter between God and the human race. Every single one of us goes through that same story again; Adam equals man, Eve equals the mother. Humanity as a whole, and each individual human being in particular, goes through this interruption in the encounter with the Living God. Humanity, for some mysterious reason, seems to want to get away from this direct meeting with God. As a result, and because mankind is what it is, something remains unfinished. To restore everything to a perfection even greater than the original, God has to enter into the affairs of the world and come to live for good among us men so that we may receive the power, beyond our own individual powers, to answer to the call of love.

Another illustration may give us more of a key to this profound mystery than a long, complicated explanation. Let's look at a certain mother and her four-year-old child. She wants to make sure that her boy has a future—as a man—about which he can't yet have the slightest idea, of course. He has no choice at this point; he has to let himself be guided and counselled by his mother. But she, on the other hand, thinks that her son must learn by degrees how to act on his own. She thinks of him as a free agent who, after being taught about things and making discoveries of his own, will be able to go his own way. Now, mother and son are together in the living room. She's mending clothes, and he's playing. He suddenly becomes interested in the empty socket of a table lamp. He climbs up on a chair and is about to poke his finger in the live socket when his mother sees this and says, "Don't touch that! . . . you'll be hurt!" She knows, of course, that he can't understand how and why he'll be hurt, but she has to count on his trust and reliance in her.

If this mother were a big worrier, a "mother hen," she would be so afraid of something bad happening now that she would take the little fellow away from the temptation, and wouldn't let him out of her sight. But this mother is by choice a real mother, who knows how to bring up her boy without coddling him. So, as she starts to leave the room she only moves the chair and repeats her warning. "Don't touch that while I'm in the kitchen, either!"

But he's still dying to touch that fascinating socket. His thinking is something like this: "What if I do go ahead and touch it anyway? . . . I want to see for myself . . . I can do it . . . Why did she say not to touch it? . . . Is there something she doesn't want me to know? . . . I can be just as smart as mother." He looks up at the socket again. He quietly pulls the chair back to the table and, with quick glances toward the kitchen door to make sure that his mother isn't coming back out again, he climbs up on the chair. And just to see what will happen, he puts his finger into the socket.

What happens happens quickly: a shock runs through his body and he falls to the floor screaming, frightened and guilty. But mostly he is upset because he feels he has been punished for his curiosity. Besides that, he has a big bump on his head from the fall. Mother has now come running in. Needless to say, she's going to scold her foolish son, but first she picks him off the floor and comforts him, puts a cool hand on his throbbing head.

If we will go beneath the surface of this incident, we'll see that it started a very important new development in the relationship between mother and son. First of all, the child has learned what might happen if he doesn't trust what his mother tells him, and he'll probably listen to her a lot more carefully in the future. He knows now that when she says "no" to something she's not just trying to interfere with his fun, but that she really wants to protect him from dangers that he can't know or understand. So, he can begin to see that she truly loves him. Secondly, he knows that he has disobeyed, but he sees that his mother has no desire to make him more ashamed and embarrassed than he is already. The opposite is true, in fact; she is doing her best to make him stop crying and feel good again.

If the child had not made his mistake, could he have discovered how deep his mother's love for him is? This question is not really a paradox. And if the mother hadn't given the child a chance to venture on his own and experiment, he wouldn't have been able to learn his own limitations. Unless she gives him freedom to learn for himself, even if it's a little painful sometimes, a mother is treating her child like a *thing*, not a *person*, like an object rather than a subject.

The mystery expressed in Chapter 3 of Genesis is something like this story of a mother and her child. What God wants for the individual, for the couple, for humanity as a whole is their destinies—and the importance of destiny surpasses freedom. God's view is infinitely greater than ours, but because our very freedom requires risk (like the mother's son) we tend to set aside God's own intent, and we try by ourselves to achieve our liberty. And so the couple Adam and Eve "put their fingers into the electrical socket." Everything went wrong. God, however, promised salvation and came *in person* to assure it, showing mankind that his love is infinite. The Eastertide liturgy sings, "*O felix culpa*; fortunate the sin which deserved a Redeemer of such quality and greatness." This is the seeming paradox of our freedom!

At this price and only this price, we discover that God wants infinitely more than just human perfection for us. He wants us to be drawn, through the mutual mingling of Christ with ourselves, into his own mysterious intimacy, into real and infinite love. Death now can be understood to be only the second and necessary stage after our birth. This way of explaining it may seem unusual, but then this *is* the main part of the whole Christian mystery.

Our existence here on earth, seen this way, begins to look like a fascinating adventure, one that breaks out to go beyond all visible limits. If we really understand what the living presence of God made flesh means to the history of mankind, we must feel that our complete agreement to his Word will give our position in the world an infinitely greater worth than we would at first have thought possible. This way we can reach toward an infinite level of life, a level we could never have known by ourselves alone. And God is so tactful that he goes to the lengths of asking us to work with him to achieve this.

Christian morality is not possible outside of this view.

What, then, does the mystery of sin mean? It is the inborn tendency within us, present well before the clear and conscious power of the will arises, to give worldly things and ideas a value that they don't really have. These worldly values—temporal values, so called—are such things as material or intellectual success, or well-organized living in the society, in a family, or in a country. A satisfying sexual life is also a temporal value. These values are positive, constructive, solid and, in many instances, completely necessary. And yet they are only relative, only preliminaries to a world that transcends them to an infinite degree. The temporal values will guide us eventually to this other, higher world, depending first on the use we make of them, but depending secondly and more importantly on whether or not we are conscious, as we use them, that they are by themselves inadequate. Sin is a sinking into the quicksand of temporal values which we mistake for absolute ones. It is a closing of one's ears to the voice of God.

The sexual expression of love is indeed, then, a basic, positive value, but it is certainly not an absolute; it is relative and impermanent. Christ made this clear when he said, in answer to the leading question put to him by the Sadducees, "For at the resurrection they are neither to marry nor to be given in marriage. . . ." Love will then no longer need to be expressed sexually; in the risen world men will be drawn into a kind of mutual relation which very much resembles—through what Saint Paul calls "adoption"—God himself, as he is in the inexpressible mystery of the Holy Trinity. And this is a way of love passing infinitely beyond the sexual.

Only God, obviously, could reveal all this to us. It isn't surprising that nations and peoples not acquainted with the Bible should always have been tempted to think mistakenly that the mystery of sexuality is a "divine" or religious reality, for the precise reason that sexuality has such a strong emotional content that it *seems* almost supernatural. And almost as often other peoples have seen sexuality as the invention of an evil god, since it was felt to be so self-contradictory and troublesome. Only our "heavenly" view can give sexual love it's true meaning.

When this is understood, a person can live correctly with sexuality in one of two ways. For one, he or she accepts the responsibility of living with another, in joint sexual relation as one married couple. Their joint sexual acts will then have twofold meaning as both the expression of love and a sharing in God's creative work. For the other, he or she may choose to ignore and rise above this worldly sexual urge. This is not in violation of man's mental and physical nature, since science recognizes now that the sexual drive does *not* require satisfaction. This second choice will bear witness, in advance, to the transcendent love of the risen world. In the one alternative, then, marriage is completely meaningful, and in the other alternative consecrated virginity is.

To return to the idea of sin, we can say in general that any kind of behavior that isn't affirmative and dynamic is essentially negative and regressive. This is really a truism, because it tells us what should be obvious, that sexual intercourse which is not intended to express the genuine love of two people for each other is thoroughly damaging—and means rejecting God's call. In a word, this is the worship of sex for itself. Saint Paul, when speaking to the Corinthians, who were Greeks, cosmopolitan Orientals steeped in pagan beliefs, always talks of idolatry in the same breath with fornication, lechery, thieving and so forth. We might remember that among these Greeks, who had a weakness for myths, secret sects and primitive notions, intercourse with the so-called sacred prostitutes was considered a religious act.

5: THOUGHTS ON MORALITY

THOUGHTS ON MORALITY

ONLY NOW, AFTER GOING OVER the fundamentals of love, can we speak of "morality" in matters of sex.

The dynamic points of Christian morality are generally very simple. Christ tells us in terms that don't leave the slightest possibility of confusion; his "command" is *love*. "Thou shalt love the Lord thy God. . . ." and *"thy neighbor* as thyself." When we think about this even a little bit, we see how far this goes as to what men are required to do—especially if we read on after this saying and find that "Upon these two commandments the whole Law hangeth, and the prophets." How can we help being startled at this bold simplicity!

Saint Paul, in his Epistle to the Romans, 13: 8-10, repeats this statement of Christ's nearly word for word, and he adds examples. If a man deceives his wife, it's because he doesn't love her enough. That much is obvious to us, but so obvious that it doesn't always get the attention it deserves, nor is it always understood clearly. Again, Saint Paul says that if a man sleeps with a prostitute he is treating a woman as if she were a piece of merchandise. This, too, is a clear example of an avoidance of the demands of real love.

We ought to put our moral concerns into our own words for our own use, based on the true moral law. This formulation of ours might become a question: "In this or that situation where I have this or that relationship with such and such a person, what must I do to bring out best the other person's value as a *subject*, as a *person*?"

Most of us couldn't put all the problems of our lives under the searching beam of such a question, and it's because the question's answer—love—is so simple that it seems too much for us. Yet love is really the only answer. But how difficult it can be! We're *always* in some kind of relationship with someone, and most of the time in a very complicated way. Also, most of these relationships actually involve more than just two people. For example, we hail a taxicab, and so become

engaged in the life of the driver. He himself is already
involved in life in certain very important ways: he's a
married man with three children, one of whom is at
the moment very sick. This is giving the father-cab-
driver a lot of worry. We don't know this, nor is there
any reason why we should know it in order to get where
we want to go in the taxicab. But we *must* realize that
we're dealing with a human being *like ourselves*, with
someone who has his own existence. And our realizing
this does make a difference in how we act with the
cabdriver, doesn't it? If we agree to look at our mode
of living this way—the only right way, according to
both psychology and the Gospel—the result is again
amazing: we can never stop having to try to love! What
this will really mean to us is a never ending exertion
on our part, constant self-denial, and an always keen
insight into things. How difficult it will be, as we meet
anyone, to never forget that that anyone is a somebody,
someone who, just like us, is standing before Christ
the Saviour, even if the someone doesn't know it!

Now, in all human affairs the situation most deeply
involving two human subjects together is having sexual
relations. This is what makes them a couple. Here, more
than anywhere else, Christ's command of love must be
the first and greatest consideration, even though the couple's sex life is actually only one part of their whole
existence together. The couple's sex life can reach its

full value only if the husband and wife each measure up to the daily requirements of their mutual love. The man, for example, who would force sexual intercourse upon his wife at a moment when she has good reason to consider it troublesome would be falling short of what love requires. His *love* for his wife is not strong enough to rise above his *urge* to possess her.

Yet, if we want to stay within the boundaries of Christian morality, sexual problems must not be the only things we think about. Sex is, after all, only one part of existence among many others. In terms of psychology, the problems of behavior created by, say, our instincts of aggression are surely as important as the problems that grow out of our sex drives. To make chastity into a fundamental virtue would be against every teaching of Christ and his Church. Saint Thomas Aquinas devotes one whole article in his *Summa theologica* to showing that chastity is *not* a cardinal virtue.

In general, it is of the greatest importance to our lives to make a distinction between the way things are and the way we think they are.

For example, to say to a fellow man "you fool!" is punishable by the fires of hell. These are Christ's own words (quoted in Matthew 5:22) and so they are the absolute, unalterable truth. We never have the right to call our neighbor a fool.

But now we get into a heated argument with a certain

contrary-minded, ill-willed opponent. We happen to get somewhat overexcited. Voices rise, tempers boil, and then we yell, "You're a fool!"

It slipped out, this insult. But it's a fact that it *was* said. We said it, we're fully aware that we said it, and we said it on purpose. If we hadn't willed to say it, we wouldn't have said it; the excuse that "it slipped" is no good. But: it is clear that our *actual moral* involvement is not as great as the *abstract* seriousness of the offense. This means that while we knew perfectly well what the Lord said, and its meaning, we didn't measure the seriousness of the break with God that this wrong act would cause, nor did we *want* the break to occur. We know that we were wrong, that it was something we mustn't do, that God is displeased; but we also fully realize now that our action went no further than mere name-calling. We did not consciously and wilfully commit ourselves to a total rejection of God and neighbor wholly and beyond recall.

It may be that we haven't yet acquired the inner calmness we need before engaging in hot discussion. Or maybe the subject of the debate was too close to our heart for us to stay cool about it. Maybe our opponent just got under our skin, how or why we don't know. If we had known we wouldn't have allowed ourselves to get into the argument with him in the first place. In brief, as soon as we realize what we've done, we simmer down. Then we can interpret our unfortunate insult as a danger signal, and as a painful reminder to try to be better the next time.

Sin—in its moral sense, not as a mystery the way it is considered in Chapter 3 of Genesis—is something that happens between real, physically real, people. *Factually*, it is all very simple: I *did* call my fellow man a fool. But the reality of this, as it is lived out by the persons actually involved, is much, much more complicated, and can't in any way just be reduced to the fact itself. All sorts of other considerations enter into the picture. In this example of the insult, there is a close, direct relationship among God, our neighbor and ourselves. Our *sin* is our position in relation to the other two, as we have acted it out. Our sin, then, depends somewhat on how responsible we feel towards these other two. It might very well be that, despite what happened, we love them both, only our will power is not well geared to this love. Probably the other two realize that the insult comes not from real malice, but only from loss of control; certainly God knows this. We may then be able, after we've calmed down, to tell the man with whom we've argued, "Look, please forget what we said a minute ago. It was wrong of us to lose our temper like that. We didn't mean what we said, you must realize that, don't you?" And we may say to God, "We've done it again! Forgive us, dear Lord! What can we do to keep our composure in the future?"

If we're sincere and tactful now, chances are good

that our opponent will forgive us. Of course, he won't be absolutely forgiveful; to err is human, for him as well as for us. Men are always touchy, as our own reactions in the argument prove only too well.

But where God is concerned, we don't have to worry at all about our forgiveness. Remember the stories of his ways with sinners: the woman caught in adultery, Mary Magdalen at Simon's table, Peter in the courtyard thrice denying knowing Christ, the thief dying on the right-hand cross at Calvary . . . God forgives even before lips have had time to open for the begging of forgiveness! God's love is infinite, without limits. Does the Prodigal Son, who had wildly and deeply broken relations with his father, even have a chance to knock at the door as he returns, repenting? No, because his father has gone far down the road to meet him. No sooner do they enter the house together than the Feast begins.

Everyday language is not always clear. Sometimes there is a confusion of terms that harms or complicates the moral and spiritual life of man, a person of good will. The confusion that interests us here is between *material act* and *formal sin*. Clearing away this confusion is necessary for good attitude and behavior in the matter of the sacraments. We shouldn't confuse the physical, social *fact* of an act with the *formal sinfulness*. This is the distinction we made in our example of the insult, too. The Sacrament of Penance isn't just for wiping out all our daily errors, nor is the Holy Eucharist a kind of approval given to all those who are "nice guys." This confusion may even lead us into sacrilege if we're not careful on this point.

To get back to the problem of sex: the first thing to keep in mind is that anything to do with sexuality is *important.* This personal power of love and creation is not to be treated as if it meant nothing, or as if it were of only secondary worth.

The younger adolescent, especially the boy, is only dimly aware that sexuality is really a procreative power. The girl usually has a quicker and deeper intuition of her potential motherhood. She soon begins to sense that there is a connection between her love for a man and her capacity to be a mother. If she were to put this feeling into words for the man, she might say, "I want your baby."

The boy develops in the opposite way. Only when he experiences true love does he realize that he's able to become a father. It is crucial for both the young man and young woman to understand just how real their creative powers are. If either one of them fails to understand this, real damage will be done to the other.

We should also keep in mind that sexual problems, like all other problems, have to be used to help along our effort toward moral progress. In Christian terms, this means the promoting of true love. Sex problems are important, to be sure, but they're still not the *most* important. More exactly, they're not the ones that set the keynote of human existence. Modern psychology clearly shows that the sex instinct can be "controlled." If we're able to balance our personality in our dealings with our fellow men, our conscience should be able to keep the lid on the sexual urges, too. The teachings of Christ hold that it is *charity*—love—that should set the keynote. The adolescent who regularly abuses himself, for example, can only free himself of that habit if he treats his "sin" as we've suggested in this chapter. He should *not* just be content to feel more and more guilty about his "sin," finally falling into a helpless despair. Rather, he should try to establish relationships of love and respect with all persons entering his daily life. He mustn't let himself dwell too strongly on purely sexual preoccupations. If he follows this program, he'll soon find that his habit will be easy to break.

In the realm of sex, so crowded with false notions and fears, nothing is more likely to prevent a truly Christian view of things than the unfortunate "taboo" feelings which are more or less the products of simple, black-and-white thinking.

In fact, these notions of "taboo" may even cause a young person to lose his faith in Christ. They can set up a conflict within the adolescent between the problems of life and the teachings of religion.

This conflict soon comes to seem like a *contradiction*, and because the young person can't solve the puzzle he "loses his faith." But what he thinks is religion's position in the problem is really *not* what religion says at all, and this misunderstanding may be mostly the fault of the adults who are responsible for the youth's religious education. If parents and teachers try to "straighten out" the youth by frightening him or making him feel guilty, the young person is liable to react in disgust by throwing off the religion that seems to be persecuting him. Actually, religion can and should actively help the adolescent to pull himself together and pass through this youthful crisis with increased respect for his religion and love for God.

Sexual problems aren't the most important moral problems. Christianity wants to expand our ability to love in all directions, and an improvement in our sexual life is only a by-product of this.

We have to learn to be at ease with ourselves by being at ease with others. A child is passive; he depends on others as from "high to low." An adult depends on others, too, but as "equal to equal," with due respect, of course, for age and position. These two attitudes are obviously worlds apart. Adolescence is the passage from the child's attitude to the adult's attitude. This change isn't easy, and it doesn't happen overnight. Sexual difficulties are only symptoms of this change, or signs that the change is being made badly.

If we continue to act like children in our day-to-day relations with others, we'll act that way with God, too.

This is where we risk losing our faith.

When we become adults our ideas of God should become less imaginative, more informed. We have to stop praying to "Little Jesus" in order to try to understand the *whole* of Christ's message. We have to replace bubbling enthusiasm with mature reflection. We learn that faith in God is not some instant dawning of light, but an often discouraging struggle that is as long and tough as life itself. But if we succeed we achieve the Kingdom of Heaven.

So the right psychological development means a mature religious outlook, and vice versa.

When we're eighteen we can't believe in the presence of Jesus in the Eucharist in the same way we did when we were ten. We have to learn to understand how the *personal* presence of the Word Incarnate is *mysterious*, much more mysterious, let's say, than the "presence" of someone we love, someone who isn't here but of whom we think and who thinks of us.

When we're eighteen we can't experience the Sacrament of Penance as we did when we were ten, either. When a boy of twenty confesses, saying, "I've disobeyed my parents, I've been a glutton, I've sinned against purity" we know right away that he's only repeating a formula that he's been taught, to which he has added his adolescent sexual problems in a wooden way that shows that he's holding everything back within himself. It's time for him to see that confession isn't just a kind of moral control exercised by a man in a black cassock, but is rather a mystical encounter with God who has come to save him and all mankind from their fundamental confusion.

Our goal here is to have knowledge of our personal relation to God. This knowledge is true and balanced only if it isn't deformed by pious exaggerations, only if it expresses itself in humility and the desire to love.

With the ideas of this section in mind, we should read over these passages in Scripture:

The First Epistle of Saint John, Chapter 3, Verses 14 to 23, and also Chapter 5, Verses 16 and 17.

Saint Paul's Epistle to the Romans, Chapter 7.

POLYGAMY

Modern psychology tells us that the normal psychological development of a human being depends upon the possibility of his or her settling into a proper married relationship.

This means that the sex instinct can be made a part of the whole personality in such a way that the sex need will fit best only in a single person-to-person relationship. If a person is married and can't keep his or her sex urges—weak or strong—under control and confined within the married life, he or she won't have a balanced personality; weaknesses will show up. This isn't merely guesswork, but a conclusion drawn from scientific observation. The key fact here is this: the more strongly the two married people can keep their sexual urges within the marriage circle, the better and stronger will be both their personalities. And the more a married person "plays around," the weaker his personality will be. And if it should happen that one of the married partners, for some reason or other, cannot have sexual intercourse, then the other partner *should* and *can* rise above the sexual urges and still keep the marriage strong and happy.

From this we must conclude that polygamy—where one husband may have many wives—isn't at all the highest level of human family relations. This isn't to say that polygamy is obviously *bad*; it simply means that polygamy is not the ideal condition for the full flowering of man's goodness or for the progress of man's personality.

Abstract reasoning is very difficult in this matter. It may be better to use comparisons with something else. These comparisons may not be perfectly exact, of course, but they can make what we're trying to see a little clearer.

Let's consider how it is with a man who does live with several wives. In the first place, it's common sense that these three or four or more people can't live as completely equal to one another. Also, the husband logically can't be *totally* pledged to each wife, and it's clear that each wife is only partly related to him, too. There can't be a relationship of mutual exchange here; the relationship is actually one of ownership, or possession. This man has several wives in the same sense that he has several pairs of shoes, or several pipes. Each wife has her own personality, which can only grow to its best and its fullest if all its inner needs are met and satisfied by a partner; but not one of the wives can possibly get this much love and attention from the shared husband.

It's interesting to see that some large parts of the Moslem world—which has traditionally practiced polygamy—are now becoming aware of these considerations. In certain areas of Islam there is a clear trend toward the emancipation and uplifting of women. This leads us to wonder, now, just what the value of a profound relation between a man and a woman is.

We believe that the *other* always is and always should be one's *equal* in the commonly shared life of marriage. But "equality" is hard to define and even harder to put fully into practice. There is always a tendency here to confuse equality with likeness. Many so-called feminist movements show, at least in part, that while some women demand *equal* rights, what they really want— often without even realizing it—is *similarity*. They want to be just like men, strong and masterful. It's not too easy to explain the precise difference between femininity and masculinity; if we try too hard, we'll make a joke out of it. But here modern psychology can help us make a realistic outline of the personality of a man and the personality of a woman.

The different physical forms of the male and the female genital systems seem to be symbolically very much like the differences that science sees between the personality of the male and that of the female. Man in the world shows forceful initiative, quick and logical perceptiveness, in a way that seems naturally to make him want to take charge of things and direct their operation. Woman's personality appears much more mysterious. She's not exactly passive—far from it—but she has an active kind of *receptiveness*. She can accept, take into herself, so to speak, what man brings to her, and she'll work it out, fashion it and form it in her own secrecy. She seems to man to be less "rational," less logical than he himself is, but her personality has rich treasures and special values which man's personality, by itself, doesn't have. It's no exaggeration that here in the world the fullest humanness can be achieved only by a man and woman joining their different values and adapting themselves to an existence together.

This mutual adaptation is just what we mean by the normal fulfilment of *sexed* relations. Earlier we saw that *sexual* relations have their full importance only within the boundaries of the mutual pledge of the married couple. And we saw the difference between *sexual*, which refers to intercourse and other forms of sex instinct, and *sexed*, which we understood then as the man accepting his special responsibilities of acting in life as a man, and the woman as a woman. We have seen now that a person's psychological maturity is actually the result of the person's fitness and capacity for *sexed* relations. Therefore the practice of polygamy in a society is always a sign of psychological immaturity and in the widest sense a lack of the civilized human values.

It's interesting to see how words uttered by Christ compare with some laws recently enacted by a new African nation as it moved forth into independence. On the one hand we have this young Moslem nation trying to legislate monogamy—marriage with only one wife— into existence; on the other hand, as related in Matthew, Chapter 19, there is Christ telling us of the oneness of the married couple and the permanence, the unchangeability of the marriage bond. In Verse 7 we read: " 'Why,' asked the Pharisees, 'then did Moses command "to give a bill of divorce and to put away"?' And He answered them, saying, 'It is because of the weakness of your fathers that Moses has allowed you to put away your wives; but in the beginning it was not so.' " We know from many historical documents, biblical and otherwise, that the Hebrew civilization and other ancient cultures of the Orient were almost all polygamous. Christ's remarks about "the weakness of your fathers" supports the very modern idea that the highest human civilization calls for the couple to be one and inseparable.

The difference between polygamy and modern divorce is slight; we can go so far as to call the difference merely one of time.

A few pages back, we mentioned a man owning shoes or pipes. Now, it is certainly all right for us to own *things* in succession, one after the other. But suppose we take a wife, and we say to ourselves, consciously or subconsciously, "If she's right for us, and everything goes well, we'll stay together, but if after a while we get tired of her we'll just get rid of her, and get another wife." Then our attitude toward the woman is almost exactly like our attitude toward automobiles: we buy one we like, owning it gives us a good feeling, it serves our needs, but when we think we've had it long enough we'll turn it in or sell it, and get a new one.

Whether a polygamous relationship is many wives at once, or many wives in succession (what we call "divorce"), it always takes the woman as a possessed *thing*, a possession.

Polyandry—one wife having several husbands at the same time—is a lot like polygamy, because a woman with several husbands (at the same time or one after the other) would also be like the owner of "things." Whatever polygamy and polyandry mean psychologically, we have to understand that both of them reflect an

113

unsatisfactory notion of the deep, living, personal relationship of marriage.

The Christian idea of marriage does no more than show how the couple must follow God's revealed views of sexuality and the created world while at the same time having the maximum *natural* consummation. Modern psychology supports this same cause, pointing out that if the child's personality is to be free and healthy the two parents must be bound together in strong and permanent harmony. We don't want to go too deeply into this idea here, except to say that where the child's personality and welfare are concerned, Christian revelation and modern psychology do not disagree about the necessity of the "oneness" of the married couple.

THE BIRTH CONTROL PROBLEM

When the adolescent gets to be fifteen or sixteen, many problems about sex come up, and they are not easy ones to solve. And although the problems aren't exactly the same for boys and for girls, they have the same general points. For boys and girls who may be already thinking—in the most unspecific way, of course—of eventual marriage, one of the most frequent questions is how to control the sex life for having children. In other words, they wonder about the pattern and the frequency of sexual intercourse, because intercourse is the part of sexuality that will bring pregnancy and childbirth. Also, the problem is now different for the young twentieth-century married couple than it was for the married couples of 150 years ago.

In those days, seventy per cent of all the newborn infants died within a few weeks. By our present-day standards of hygiene and preventive medicine, such a high figure is shocking. But this figure hides a very practical fact about those days: if a couple then wanted to have four or five surviving children, the hard facts of life forced them to "produce" from ten to twelve infants. Nowadays, though, infant mortality (or infant death rate) has been cut down to an amazingly low 1.5 per cent by medical advances. This now gives the death of a tiny infant the same touch of tragedy that surrounds the untimely death of a twenty-five-year-old man or woman. This improvement has had tremendous consequences in many ways, but here we should look only at its impact on the young couple at the start of their married life, as they ask themselves how they're going to regulate their sexual life.

Let's keep looking at cold figures for a while. Suppose a girl married at twenty. Her generative life, her active production of eggs, will last until she is fifty years old, more or less. Theoretically, she can have a child every eighteen months; this is not a physical impossibility. At this rate, if she "let nature take its course," she could very well have a total of twenty-five pregnancies in her lifetime. Infant mortality being as low as it is these days, chances are very good that she would be the mother of twenty-two living children. This is the basic problem facing every modern couple, only shown in the extreme, and expressed theoretically.

Beyond a doubt, the fight against infant death has scored great victories. But this also means that married people will have greater and greater problems to constantly, intelligently and of their own free will *manage* their fertility. They have to learn how to space the births of their children. The modern couple can no longer, as in the past, give nature a free rein. Control of births in the old days meant, in practice, letting death be the agent of natural selection in the many ways which had not been blocked, as they now are, by advancing medical science. Maybe the lowered infant death rate isn't the only reason for the rising birth rate throughout our modern world, but it's certainly one of the most important.

The conclusion is this: modern couples, far more than the couples of yesteryear, have the obligation of facing up squarely to the problem of regulating births. Man and wife of course want to remain faithful to their human and Christian ideals, but they must fit *how many* children they will have, and *when*, to their ability to provide proper upbringing and education to these children.

If we concentrate our view upon the couple just as Christians, we'll have the idea that they're called upon by God, in a special way, to give to the world—humanity as redeemed by Christ, forming the Mystical Body—as many other human beings as they can. But these new human beings should be brought up to reach eventually the highest possible degree of natural perfection. Whether or not the child will be able to get such an upbringing will essentially be determined by the particular situation of each couple.

Here is an important point, and one that needs special emphasis. Suppose that a couple have an "only child," and that they firmly planned to have *only* this one child. Modern psychology tells us that this child will pick up from his parents this attitude of theirs, a cramped, narrow, selfish attitude. This only child will, more often than not, show some signs of a psychological lack. He will very often become a not-too-well-adjusted adult, not quite self-fulfilled, always troubled with problems in getting along with other people. At the other extreme, some children of over-large families (and these do exist!) will show very similar abnormal tendencies when they are examined psychologically. To have too large a family is not, of course, the expression of the parents' selfishness, but it is perhaps the sign of poor self-control and not enough care for the development of the children as individual personalities.

In this modern day and age, then, the couple ought,

by real necessity, to control voluntarily and practically the coming of its children. This controlling is variously known as family planning, planned parenthood, spacing of births, *birth control*. There is no question the modern husband and wife are under this obligation, so as to be able to carry out their God-given vocation in the best possible way. An idea of marriage which would consider nothing else as right except having the greatest possible number of children would certainly not be Christian. The problem of the birth and upbringing of children requires a great amount of prudence. A fair proportion should be set between the marital activity of the couple and what the best things for the family really and practically are. This kind of thinking is common for all other areas of human life, so why shouldn't we use it in connection with the fertility of the married couple, too?

How touchy this problem is begins to show up when we start to consider the actual practical means of achieving birth control. Obviously the *only absolutely sure* way of not having children is to have no sexual intercourse. But this is simple only in theory. In human beings, beings with spirituality and conscience, the sexual act is not *only* good for reproduction. Since the distant past, people have found many different ways to block the fertility of sexual intercourse. The basic requirement for this is simple: to put between the man and the woman having intercourse something designed to block the normal results of the act. There are physical means and chemical means of barring the entry of the spermatozoa into the uterus, and there are means of destroying them before they can meet the ovum. Without a doubt the oldest method of birth control is the one used by Onan, as described in the Bible itself. This consists in cutting short the sexual act before the man's seed can be projected into the woman's genital passages. Whatever the means of contraception used, we ought to give some thought to the deep implications of using some such method. Suppose that at the moment when a woman is physiologically ready to be impregnated, a contraceptive procedure—to prevent conception—is followed; the fact is that the man and the woman are acting out a contradiction here. They're engaging in an activity of extreme emotional and physiological complexity, but at the very moment when this action is leading up to fertilization, its natural climax, its course is interrupted by a foreign element, the contraceptive. We must feel, as the man and woman "take" each other in this way, that they are twisting each other's dignity as prospective father and mother. With a contraceptive device, the sexual encounter loses the qualities of total, mutual giving and receiving. Such a sexual relation is certainly not the genuine and positive expression of real love. We can fully understand the Church's regular reminders that any sexual conduct done in such a way as to prevent the full completion of the sexual purpose is flatly opposed to the demands of Christian love.

Now let's look at a husband and wife who, for some reason, are absolutely unable to have children. As they have intercourse, it can only be for one of its two purposes: the expression of their love for each other. They take each other, and offer themselves to each other as they are, without any restrictions. It's not their fault that their sexual act can't be productive, since even the greatest surge of their will to have a child won't make this possible. And this is exactly the situation that occurs in every couple when the woman's genital life has passed away at her change of life. This is also the situation with younger couples during the time in a woman's period when she's absolutely incapable of being impregnated, the time from about the third day *after* ovulation until the next menstrual flow. Intercourse under these conditions where the woman cannot possibly be made pregnant is basically different from a sexual act purposely spoiled while performed during a time when the woman *can* be impregnated.

But a couple might do the following: when they marry, they might fall into a petty self-centeredness and decide to have no children, or anyway fewer children than they could really afford to raise and educate. Let's suppose, too, that they very carefully respect the laws of the Church about sex, to the letter of that law, and so they think they are "avoiding sin." So of course they won't use contraceptives, but they *will* limit their sexual relations strictly to those moments when the wife cannot be fertilized. Contrary to what they may think, they are being fundamentally sinful, because they are deliberately refusing to meet the demands of child-bearing that are normal for their particular married situation. They can afford to have children, but they won't.

When we look at a normal couple, however, one that wants to have children as the family's situation, financial and otherwise, allows, we see something entirely different. This pair, also, are against the practice of contraceptive sexual relations, and they too limit their sexual intercourse to the periods of non-fertility. They are also determined to show and increase their mutual love, *but* they in no way show the attitude of basic selfishness that the other couple does. Because they're able to space their sexual acts taking into account *both* the wife's cycle of fertility *and* their planned and practical capacity to support children, they prove that they've both reached a really desirable degree of psychological balance. This means that their love has been strong enough to overcome the conflict we discussed in the last chapter; their erotic urges don't overpower their feelings and their self-control. This is one of the extremely important aspects of conjugal life. The young couple shouldn't be carried away with some kind of sexual rapture, and yet this is always a possibility, perhaps because of some lingering adolescent attitudes. From the human standpoint as well as from the Christian standpoint, the couple will be doing best to think about the rhythm of the woman's fertility (if it is familiarly known) from the very beginning of their life together, in order to control their sexual relationship.

On this point, modern medicine and biology are able to give us very enlightening information. Scientific advances, by reducing infant mortality, raised many new problems of conscience for married people. But, interestingly enough, other scientific developments, inspired by these new difficulties, have enabled modern woman to know herself and her ovarian rhythm with a certainty unheard of in the past. There are certain clues that will enable her to tell when she is in one phase of her ovarian activity and when in another. If a woman observes and understands these signs she can know with fair accuracy just how her ovarian system is operating, just as in much the same way it is possible for any person to understand and control the passing of wastes out of the body, for example. It is ideal if a young girl can learn to read these signs of her ovarian activity as soon as possible after her menstrual flows have settled into a pattern. This will enable her to enter married life, later, with a full knowledge of herself.

We should finish this section by restating a fact that ought to be obvious: there is no moral perfection in the matter of birth control. The physiological and spiritual development of the human person are never in fact wholly complete. But there is an *adequate* response to the call of God, and it depends on the overall attitude and the dynamic principles of the couple's life, judged in the light of God's call. The successful blending of sexual life with all other phases of married life must enable the couple to do without contraceptive practices. But the married couple certainly can't be expected to create such harmony in their very first few days of life together. What is far more important morally is the general—but personal—attitude of the couple who strive always toward the ideal. In this young couple the love that flows between them will be ever more truly human, and ever closer to what God expects of them both.

FLIRTING—AND PETTING

The meaning of the word "flirting" isn't clear right away. Everyone will agree that a certain kind of flirting is bad, but that another kind is good.

If it means a boy's first attempts to attract the attention of girls, to test his charm and desirability and parade his new masculinity, then flirting might well be harmless.

Most of the time, however, what we call flirting is very different from this. Usually it is nothing else, in whatever disguise, than a sexual game between boy and girl, involving definite erotic excitement but stopping short of any actual final fulfillment. We call this kind of flirting *petting*.

This is a very rough definition, of course, but when understood in its dangerous sense (as it usually is when people criticize it) flirting reveals an adolescent attitude, a poorly controlled sexual instinct. Seen as adolescent in nature, it is simply *self*-erotic excitation fed with real sensations instead of mere fancies of the imagination. The partner in a flirtation of this bad sort is marked down in value, becoming just a pleasure-giving thing.

This sexual game not only doesn't involve any real human relationship, but actually prevents such a relationship. Generally speaking, no young man would want for a minute to have the girl with whom he is currently flirting to be his wife, his life companion, the mother of his children. We don't have to go far to find the great drawbacks of this kind of flirting. We should remember what we said in earlier chapters about the training of the sexual instinct; we can understand that flirting only serves to prolong adolescent attitudes in a person's behavior.

For Christianity, petting is clearly in direct conflict with love, because Christian love must be mutual. Petting is opposed to charity. It also shows that the sexual instinct has not been integrated into the whole personality, and, more than that, that the person has given up all efforts to make progress toward such maturity.

But how about flirting in the good sense, when young people want simply to know more about the world of the opposite sex? How about these youthful boy-girl relations, unmarked by self-erotism? These are good; in fact they are quite necessary overtures from the innocent male world to the equally innocent world of females. Foolishly difficult obstacles thrown between boys and girls would be unnatural and undesirable. It is absolutely necessary for boys and girls to know about each other. Unnecessary obstacles would probably lead young people into trying to become acquainted in secret, which would only give them a sense of guilt and would certainly not help them lead a healthier life as adults.

CELIBACY

Celibacy refers to when a person, unmarried, has not pledged his or her life to being one with a specific person of the other sex, and doesn't expect to do so. This situation may contain a number of different psychological attitudes. There is the boy, for example, who is not yet securely enough established in society to assume the responsibilities of running a family. Again, there is the man of forty or fifty, the basically selfish fellow who never did want to assume the burden of responsibility for a family, who never wanted to be bothered by a wife and children, and who prefers to live the well-organized but petty life of a bachelor. This is the "old boy." There is also the young lady who, for a number of reasons—and this is a very complicated and delicate situation—has not been able to find the life-mate she deeply yearns for.

Finally, there are persons, fully mature adults, who don't enter married life only because they find some other way of life that leads them to an even wider human social activity.

This is not mere bachelorhood or spinsterhood, which have a very narrow social significance. For instance, a man who lives with a woman is nevertheless nothing more than a celibate, unless this union is made socially stable—by marriage. The word "celibacy" has nothing to do directly with the sexual activity of the celibate person; some celibates may have considerable sex activity, while other celibates may indulge in none at all. This first kind of celibate, generally, is just continuing to act like a self-centered adolescent. The old bachelor is often a man who hasn't had the strength of will to commit himself deeply, once and for all, to living. He remains a more or less withdrawn character, shy as far as involvement in married life is concerned. He tends to look for compensation in brief sentimental or erotic affairs.

Very different is the kind of celibate who has freely chosen to pass by the call of marriage so that he can engage in a much wider field of human interests. This will only be possible, according to modern psychology, if the person has grown normally to full emotional maturity. We've already seen that the sexual instinct, unlike the so-called aggressive instincts, is *not* one of man's absolutely basic needs. It does, it is true, represent each individual's interest in his species, but sexual satisfaction isn't really essential to the balance and well-being of the individual himself. When all things have found their best level, and when the emotions have matured, a person should be able to override the tensions of his sexual needs.

In this sense we can say that celibacy is psychologically justifiable *only* if it expresses the actions of an emotionally mature person. This means that if the person is capable of fully pledging himself to married life, then he or she should also be able to go even further, to give oneself to others in a way that goes beyond the satisfactions of the normal sexual life.

This way is usually the celibacy of religious dedication. We should make clear the consecrated celibacy—or in this case chastity—which is part of the character of those religious persons, the priest and the nun. The pledge of religious vows, for them, is an entrance into a way of life in which their rising above sexual needs bears witness to the supernatural source of human love and sexuality. But a life of permanent chastity is not the essential part of the priesthood. We can easily conceive that a man may have the power to celebrate the mystery of the Eucharist, to dispense the Lord God's sacraments, and still lead the life of a married man. The Eastern Rites of the Catholic Church allow this, in fact. Celibacy in the priesthood only reflects a Church law, particularly in the Roman Catholic Church, which assumes that the mysteries of the priesthood require so much of the person's energies that it seems desirable that he should not marry, and thus save his strength all for the priesthood. This view is reinforced by quite a few psychological, mystical and practical reasons. But to repeat: marriage and priesthood are not *in themselves* incompatible. In practice, however, we see that the religious state itself—whether of an ordained priest or nun or not—must usually mean that the person will make the choice to renounce sexual practices.

So we can see that the priesthood and consecrated religious life demand at least as much emotional maturity as married life does. It would certainly be both false and harmful to believe in any way that the celibacy of priests and other religious people is only an escape from the responsibilities and hardships of sex and marriage.

On the contrary; besides getting married, the only way a man or woman of normal psychological growth can give the personality its fullest use is to offer his or her whole being to all other human beings. In this way they can act out their faith with *every* person they meet.

BY WAY OF CONCLUSION

BY WAY OF CONCLUSION

IN MANKIND'S NEVER ENDING SEARCH for confidence and happiness, the "problems of sex," as they are often called, are important, but they are not so important that they overshadow all other concerns. Young people, growing and developing, often fall into the mistake of making too much of the problems of sex. They either blow these problems up into a whole world of trouble, or else, ignorant of sex but at the same time reacting against other people's narrow-mindedness, they underestimate them.

Ignorance is *not* the way gradually to master and control one's own vital forces, as experience proves again and again. This little book was made to be a weapon, however imperfect, in the fight against ignorance of sexual matters.

We all agree that morality is the controlled effort of each human being to reach the highest degree of humanness and understanding. But we of course ought to have the right idea about just what "humanness and understanding" really mean. Man's sciences, especially biology and psychology, have by their discoveries broadened and deepened these meanings. They have been able to cast a great amount of light upon what was already known about man and his destiny from God's revelation. We shouldn't be overly optimistic, maybe, but it does seem that young people of today have open to them all kinds of information that has never before been available to youth.

Hopefully this book will help young people to know and use the forces of human dignity and love as we see these forces through modern scientific knowledge and through God's revealed word. Each young man and woman needs instruction in spiritual self-denial in order to bring the drives of sexual instinct into line with the attitudes of "togetherness" that we need for married life. Self-denial is a matter of personal choice, but this choice and the subsequent moral effort should certainly be made a lot easier by the fact that enlightenment now comes from two different sources: faith and science. These two, each supporting the other, can dispel anxiety, clarify what is happening, and give us some idea of things to come.

A LIST FOR FURTHER READING

ADVICE FOR YOUTH

BOWDERN, WILLIAM. *Problems of Courtship and Marriage*. St. Louis: Queen's Work.

GUARNERO, LOUISA. *The Wonder of Growing Up*. New York: All Saints Press.

KELLY, GEORGE A. *The Catholic Youth's Guide to Love and Life*. New York: Random House.

KELLY, GERALD. *Modern Youth and Chastity*. St. Louis: Queen's Work.

McCARTHY, RAPHAEL C. *Grow Up and Marry*. St. Louis: Queen's Work.

MEYER, FULGENCE. *Safeguards of Chastity*. Cincinnati: St. Francis Shop. An instruction for young men.

———. *Helps to Purity*. Cincinnati: St. Francis Shop. An instruction for young women.

———. *Youth's Pathfinder*. Cincinnati: St. Francis Shop. Chats on vocation, love, courtship and marriage.

PIRE, LIONEL E. *The Heart of a Young Man, or Talks on Personal Purity to Boys*. New York: Frederick Pustet.

135

GUIDES TO SEX EDUCATION

HALEY, JOSEPH E. *Accent on Purity: A Guide to Sex Education*. Notre Dame: Fides Publishers.

KELLY, AUDREY A. *A Catholic Parent's Guide to Sex Education*. New York: Hawthorn Books.

KELLY, GEORGE A. *Your Child and Sex: A Guide for Catholic Parents*. New York: Random House.

LORD, DANIEL A. *Some Notes for the Guidance of Youth*. St. Louis: Queen's Work.

SATTLER, HENRY V. *Parents, Children and the Facts of Life*. Garden City, New York: Doubleday.

INDEX

Index by Lyn Hayes Editorial Service

THE AUTHOR AND HIS BOOK

MARC ORAISON *was born in 1914 at Ambares in the Gironde district of France. First becoming a doctor of medicine at the University of Bordeaux, he later became a priest and then a doctor of theology at the University of Paris. His medical vocation has taken him as far as Indochina, where he was in the French Army Medical Corps during the days just before the fall of Dienbienphu. For more than ten years now, Doctor Oraison has been doing research in new areas of psychology, and at present lives in Paris. He began writing in 1952, and several of his books have appeared in the United States, among them* Illusion and Anxiety *(Macmillan, 1963)*, Man and Wife *(Macmillan, 1962)*, Love or Constraint? *(Paulist Press), and* Love, Sin and Suffering *(Macmillan, 1964)*.